The Thoughtful Reader in the Primary School

UKRA Teaching of Reading Monographs

Advisory editors 1977–
Asher Cashdan, Head of Department of Communication Studies
Sheffield City Polytechnic
Alastair Hendry, Principal Lecturer in Primary Education
Craigie College of Education

Listening to Children Reading
Helen Arnold

The Thoughtful Reader in the Primary School
Elizabeth Wilson

Advisory editor to the series (1971–7)
John E. Merritt, Professor of Educational Studies,
The Open University, Milton Keynes

Reading Readiness
John Downing and Derek Thackray

Reading, Writing and Relevance
Mary Hoffman

Modern Innovations in the Teaching of Reading
Donald Moyle and Louise M. Moyle

Reading: Tests and Assessment Techniques
(new edition in preparation)
Peter D. Pumfrey

Reading and the Consumer
Alma Williams

Print and Prejudice
Sarah Goodman Zimet (with an additional chapter by Mary Hoffman)

The Thoughtful Reader in the Primary School

Elizabeth Wilson

Hodder and Stoughton
In association with the United Kingdom Reading Association

British Library Cataloguing in Publication Data

Wilson, Elizabeth
    The thoughtful reader in the primary school.
    1. Reading (elementary).
    I. Title
    372.4   LB1573
ISBN 0 340 26295 8

First published 1983
Copyright © 1983 Elizabeth Wilson

Photoset by Rowland Phototypesetting Ltd
Bury St Edmunds, Suffolk
Printed and bound for
Hodder and Stoughton Educational,
a division of Hodder and Stoughton Ltd,
Mill Road, Dunton Green, Sevenoaks, Kent,
by St Edmundsbury Press
Bury St Edmunds, Suffolk

Contents

Acknowledgments

I am grateful for the help I have received from many people in the preparation of this monograph, particularly from the pupils and staff of St Annes County Primary School, Lancashire and Hookstone Chase County Primary School, North Yorkshire, and from Asher Cashdan and Alastair Hendry for their constructive criticisms of this work.

I would also like to thank Donald Moyle and the late Jean Ainslie, Edge Hill College of Higher Education, for their support and encouragement in the study of the teaching of reading, and all those at home and at the primary schools I attended as a child, Malvern Way Infants School and Little Green Junior Mixed School, Hertfordshire, who worked so hard to teach me to read.

Harrogate, 1983   *Elizabeth Wilson*

The author and publisher would like to thank the Oxford University Press for permission to reproduce the extract on pages 49–50 from *Oxford Junior English 4* by Oliver Gregory, 1974 © Oliver Gregory, and Science Research Associates (Canada) Ltd, © 1969 by Science Research Associates (Canada) Ltd, and SRA Ltd, and SRA Pty Ltd, for the article on pages 62–5.

Introduction

Few people in our society today would dispute the fact that it is important to learn to read. The majority of five-year-olds entering school expect to learn to read; but exactly what is it that they should be learning? The most effective reading we can help children to achieve must surely be what may be termed 'thoughtful reading'. This is far more than being able to 'read' words in the sense of looking at printed words and pronouncing them correctly; it involves comprehension of what is read. However, 'thoughtful reading' is more than a passive type of comprehension in which the reader understands what is written without further reflection. 'Thoughtful reading' is a kind of two-way communication between author and readers; the readers bring their own ideas and knowledge to the reading, using them to help gain an understanding of what is read and to evaluate the ideas and information put forward by the author; having abstracted and evaluated the relevant ideas and information readers then go on to make appropriate use of the material they have read.

Learning to read effectively and thoughtfully is important because it can satisfy four main human needs:

functional literacy;
self-concept;
freedom of thought;
recreation.

Modern society is organised in such a way that people need to be able to read to function adequately and independently. There are numerous notices to read, forms to fill in, and instructions to follow, which fluent readers process almost automatically, but which can prove to be very real difficulties for less fluent or non-readers. Inability to read these everyday items can give rise to severe difficulties in functioning in society both at home and at work. If there were no pictures, how could a non-reader select the required items at the supermarket? How difficult it must be for non-readers to follow road signs, or to know which bus to get on. Life must be a constant struggle to overcome this handicap of being unable to read.

We also need to be able to read because our society expects it. Inadequate readers often feel the need to try to hide their reading difficulties because of a sense of embarrassment or shame. It is strange, but nonetheless true, that people are willing to admit to being poor spellers or poor mathematicians, but few would admit as willingly that they are poor readers. From the time children begin school, or even before, the pressure is on them from parents and peers to learn to read, and to learn to read as quickly and as well as everyone else.

In a democratic society freedom of thought is of great importance. Each individual member of society needs to be able to choose what will be read and to be able to bring a thoughtful, critical mind to that reading. If people were not 'thoughtful readers', the writers of propaganda could have tremendous influence on society and our whole social system could be changed at the whim of a few; advertisers could persuade people to buy things they really did not want on an even larger scale than they do already.

There is great scope for the use of reading as a recreational activity, either directly in reading material such as novels, or indirectly in reading instructions to carry out another recreational activity. Now, when people have increasing amounts of leisure time, reading can be a valuable resource.

In primary schools we have the responsibility of developing the early reading abilities of children. The way in which this is done is likely to have a strong influence on their efficiency as adult readers, and also on their attitudes towards reading. In this monograph the main processes, attitudes, strategies and skills needed by 'thoughtful readers' are described together with a number of reading activities for primary school children. In Chapter 1 the major aspects of the process of thoughtful reading, as they are at present understood, are described. One difficulty for fluent readers who wish to help beginners is that they cannot analyse exactly how they themselves read; the process has long been so automatic that they do not really know how they read. This chapter tries to show something of what goes on inside people's heads as they read, for the most part taking the fluent reader as the model since this is what our teaching is aiming at, but also describing some of the differences of approach between beginners and fluent readers.

Of course people do not always read in the same way. Some variation in reading strategy is often called for by different types of reading tasks. In Chapter 2, by classifying reading tasks according to four criteria:

    the purpose of the reader;
    the type of reading material being used;
    the purpose of the author;
    the skills and techniques needed by the reader,
teachers may be helped to provide children with a balance of different types of reading, calling for different reading strategies and skills.

Thoughtful reading is not a mechanical skill but a process involving the whole intellect and personality. In the third chapter the characteristics of people which seem to bear a close relationship to thoughtful reading are discussed. It seems clear that children's reading development cannot be separated from their general development of personality, attitudes, and general communication skills.

Chapter 4 looks at the influence of the teacher. Parents often comment on the influence teachers have, intentionally or unintentionally, on their children's ideas and attitudes; some of the ways teachers influence children as they learn to read are discussed in this chapter. Methods of diagnosing children's difficulties and ways of organising the teaching are also described.

Finally a variety of reading activities are included and their value in helping children to become 'thoughtful readers' is discussed. It is hoped that teachers will find these ideas useful in devising teaching programmes to help children become readers who not only *can* but also *do* read independently and effectively to meet their own individual needs.

1 Four aspects of the process of thoughtful reading

No one has, as yet, been able fully to describe and explain the way in which a reader is able to ascribe meaning to a written text. The process of reading is a highly complex one, involving many characteristics of the reader as well as of the text. Because of this it may well be the case that the reading process is slightly different for each individual reader, even though they may all be considered to be fluent readers reading the same text. In view of this complexity and variability of the reading process it would not be appropriate to attempt to set out here a model of the reading process; instead of this it would seem to be more helpful to consider a number of aspects of the reading task in an attempt to highlight those which are of particular importance for teachers to bear in mind.

Four main aspects of the process of thoughtful reading will be discussed:

(1) purpose for reading;
(2) the inter-relationship of types of skill for word recognition;
(3) reading skills at paragraph level;
(4) differences between beginning readers and fluent readers.

Whilst isolating each aspect for the purposes of discussion, all four need to be taken into account by the teacher for any really effective instruction to take place. Purpose for reading is discussed first since this is the logical starting point for a reading task and the type of reading and thinking most appropriate may vary according to the purpose for reading. Word recognition skills have traditionally been taught early in the primary school and these are discussed next. However, although thoughtful reading needs efficient word recognition skills, it is not suggested that these should be taught in isolation or before a child is helped to consider the meaning and relevance of a text. The third aspect of the process is of great importance since the 'thoughtful reader' must by definition be able to comprehend and think about what is read. Fourthly, some of the differences between the beginning reader and the fluent reader are considered in order to enable teachers to formulate realistic expectations of the children they teach and to have some understanding of the way in which children's reading skills may develop.

1 Four aspects of the process of thoughtful reading

No one has, as yet, been able fully to describe and explain the way in which a reader is able to ascribe meaning to a written text. The process of reading is a highly complex one, involving many characteristics of the reader as well as of the text. Because of this it may well be the case that the reading process is slightly different for each individual reader, even though they may all be considered to be fluent readers reading the same text. In view of this complexity and variability of the reading process it would not be appropriate to attempt to set out here a model of the reading process; instead of this it would seem to be more helpful to consider a number of aspects of the reading task in an attempt to highlight those which are of particular importance for teachers to bear in mind.

Four main aspects of the process of thoughtful reading will be discussed:

(1) purpose for reading;
(2) the inter-relationship of types of skill for word recognition;
(3) reading skills at paragraph level;
(4) differences between beginning readers and fluent readers.

Whilst isolating each aspect for the purposes of discussion, all four need to be taken into account by the teacher for any really effective instruction to take place. Purpose for reading is discussed first since this is the logical starting point for a reading task and the type of reading and thinking most appropriate may vary according to the purpose for reading. Word recognition skills have traditionally been taught early in the primary school and these are discussed next. However, although thoughtful reading needs efficient word recognition skills, it is not suggested that these should be taught in isolation or before a child is helped to consider the meaning and relevance of a text. The third aspect of the process is of great importance since the 'thoughtful reader' must by definition be able to comprehend and think about what is read. Fourthly, some of the differences between the beginning reader and the fluent reader are considered in order to enable teachers to formulate realistic expectations of the children they teach and to have some understanding of the way in which children's reading skills may develop.

As primary school teachers it is important that our teaching should be based on the present needs of the children, in terms of necessary skills and knowledge to be learned and their enjoyment of reading, and also on the long-term goals of producing readers who, as adults, are able to deal effectively with any reading task they may need to undertake. It is all too easy for a teacher to become absorbed in the week's or term's work and forget the overall goal of the teaching, which the individual teacher will probably not have the opportunity of seeing achieved as the child grows up and leaves school. Therefore, in order to set the teaching of the primary school child in perspective, some ways in which a fluent adult reader approaches a text will be considered here, so that we may ensure that the teaching children receive in their primary schools is designed to promote the most effective strategies and habits for reading.

1 Purpose for reading

Adult readers always read for their own purposes. On each occasion they may have a different purpose, for example, in reading a detective story to find out 'who done it', or reading a set of instructions to find out how to use a new gadget. The circumstances in which the reading takes place may also affect the purpose for reading, as when someone in a dentist's waiting-room reads a magazine, not because the content of the magazine is particularly interesting, but simply to avoid thinking about the dental treatment.

Part of learning to read is discovering the variety of purposes for reading. It is extremely important that from the earliest stages a child appreciates why it is worth while learning to read. Before they enter school most children will have seen people reading to fulfil a wide variety of purposes, from reading stories aloud to the child to reading the labels on tins and packets in the supermarket, from reading the programmes to be broadcast on television to reading the instructions for a new game. The experiences of the children will be very different, but all except a small minority of children will come to school with some ideas about why people read.

Just as in adult reading the purpose for reading has a definite influence on the type of reading that takes place and the outcomes of that reading for the individual reader, so purpose in reading also influences the attitudes and learning of the child. If children are presented with a reading situation in which they can see little purpose, they are unlikely to devote as much energy and attention to the task as they would if they could appreciate that the task had a purpose which was directly relevant to them.

Purposeful reading tasks are also important in the development of the child's understanding of what reading is, how people use reading, and how the child himself could learn to use reading. The pre-school experiences of children will be very varied: some will come to school with a clear idea of what reading is, and may already be beginning to read for themselves; others will have had fewer opportunities to learn about reading and may even enter school with adverse attitudes towards reading. Perhaps one of the first and most important tasks of the teacher of young children is to help them to see reading as something worth-while for them to learn to do for themselves, and something which can be used to satisfy a variety of needs.

In the daily organisation of the classroom there are many opportunities for purposeful reading activities to take place. The children enjoy listening to the teacher read a story to them, and through this have clearly demonstrated to them one of the uses of reading. Five-year-olds entering school can see the purpose of being able to read their own names in order to find the correct pegs to hang their coats on. They can see the purpose of having labels on cupboards so that they and the teacher can quickly find a particular piece of equipment.

Difficulties in ensuring that reading instruction is purposeful become more noticeable as more formal instruction begins. The problem is that what may be a purposeful activity in the eyes of the teacher may not have the same purpose, or even any purpose at all, in the eyes of the child. The teaching situations in which this may be most likely to occur are those in which the teacher sets out to teach one aspect or small part of the reading process. In the early stages this might be a particular letter or sound, or, at a later stage, the skill of skimming or scanning. By the teacher's very act of producing a clear-cut objective for teaching, a skill may be isolated from its context in the total reading process to such an extent that the child is uncertain of the reason for learning the particular skill. Whilst the teacher may have a clear understanding of the purposes for teaching and may have thought out the lesson very carefully, the child may see no purpose in the task at all, or may consider the purpose to be to please the teacher rather than to learn the skill because it is needed for reading.

It is, of course, possible to plan that the teacher's and the child's purposes in an activity will be different. An example of this is the reading game designed to help a child to learn particular sight words or a certain phonic rule. The teacher's purpose is that the child should learn the sight words or the phonic rule; the child's purpose may include the teacher's purpose, but the child's main purpose is to win the game.

In most classrooms the teacher and pupil purposes set for the various activities probably overlap to a sufficient degree for adequate learning to take place. The danger lies in the situation in which children can see either no purpose at all in the activity or actively reject the teacher's purpose. Fortunately the latter of these situations is fairly uncommon; however, the former is probably more widespread than we would care to admit. As teachers we must constantly be checking that the activities provided for the children have definite purposes which they can understand and accept.

If a child is trying to co-operate with the teacher but does not understand why a certain skill or fact should be learned, then learning will probably suffer in two ways:

(a) motivation to learn will be reduced, and so learning will be less efficient;

(b) when the fact or skill has been learned, the child may be unable to apply it in another situation.

Clearly the task of teaching is only half done if we teach a child a skill but do not also ensure that that skill can be used in the appropriate situations.

Purpose, as well as affecting motivation and attention, also has a direct influence on reading strategies used and reading outcomes. A person who reads a novel as a leisure activity will have a very different reading approach and final understanding and impression of the book from the student who is reading the same novel to study the literary style of the author. In the case of non-fiction texts, one person may be reading to gain an overall impression of the information presented in the text, whereas another person may be reading to discover one small item of information; because of their different purposes the two readers need different reading strategies if they are to read efficiently. Through the introduction of a variety of purposes for reading, teachers can demonstrate to their pupils that there is more than one way to read a text.

If the various reading strategies are taught in relation to definite and relevant purposes for reading, it is more likely that the child will be able to transfer the learning to other similar situations, since the pupil will learn not only a number of reading strategies but also the contexts in which they are appropriate. Merritt (1974) has suggested five main areas in which human purposes are exercised. A discussion of these and their relevance to the teaching of reading may be found below (page 19).

In schools the teaching of reading has traditionally been mainly through the medium of fictional materials, implying that the main purpose for reading is recreational. However, children are quick to notice the uses for reading in the world around them. When seven-year-olds are asked what they think they will use their reading for after leaving school they often say 'to get a job' although they may be uncertain exactly what the job will be. One boy in my class thought that he would need to pass a test to get a job, and he thought it would be important to be able to read the questions. Other ideas are often very functional, for example, 'to make sure you take the right turning off the motorway' and 'so that you can pick up the right packets and tins at the supermarket'. Another interesting response o. made by children is that they ought to learn to read because it is something that all adults do, or they would feel silly if they could not read. Clearly children see reading skill as a status symbol.

2 The inter-relationship of types of skill for word recognition

There are four basic types of skill used by readers for word recognition:
  sight vocabulary – the ability to recognise whole words;
  phonics – the use of letter-sound relationships;
  syntax – the use of grammatical context;
  semantics – the understanding of word and phrase meanings.
Beginning readers are usually more involved with the marks on the page or 'surface structure' than are fluent readers, who have become so practised in the decoding of words that they are able to pay far less attention to this and are free to direct more of their attention to the meaning suggested by the print, the 'deep structures' of the text.

But if these skills are named in a list of this kind, it is all too easy to consider them in isolation from one another, as if they were discrete skills having no influence upon one another. However, if our aim is to help children to become mature, fluent readers, we do them a disservice by separating these skills for teaching. The fluent reader uses all these skills to read a text, switching from one to another at great speed as he ascribes meaning to the print. The way readers use these skills is probably determined largely by their previous experience and knowledge of the subject matter, their familiarity with the vocabulary and the sentence structures used. For example, if fluent readers find the material easy to read, that is they have previously read all the words many times and are familiar with their meanings, they have a good knowledge of the subject being discussed, and the sentence structures are simple for them to follow, then they will pay far less attention to the graphic information presented by the words on the page and far more to the author's meaning and their own interpretation and opinion of the ideas conveyed by the print. If, on the other hand, readers are unfamiliar with the subject matter or vocabulary, or the sentence structures are complicated, then they will find themselves paying more attention to the surface structure of the text and may become conscious of using phonic skills which are normally so automatic as to be unnoticed.

It is impossible to read any text effectively using only one type of reading skill, for example, the use of phonics without attention to syntax and semantics can cause difficulty in deciding whether a word such as 'read' is in the present or past tense; the word 'lead' could be a heavy mineral, or a strip of leather attached to a dog's collar – and there are many other examples of differing pronunciation of words according to their meaning, even though the spelling remains the same.

At the other end of the spectrum, an over-reliance on meaning can also produce inaccuracies in reading, for example, the child who reads 'boat' for 'ship' in the sentence, 'He sailed away in his ship.' In a case like this the child is trying to make sense of the text, but is probably relying heavily on earlier parts of the story and clues given in pictures in the book.

Efficient readers use a constantly varying combination of skills for reading, the process having become so automatic that they are rarely aware of it as they read. They are probably able to recognise numerous words on sight, but the recognition of these words is aided by phonic cues, particularly of first letters and endings, and by the context in which words are found. They use phonics with great skill, recognising common spelling patterns and more difficult ones such as 'ough' without giving great attention to each individual letter before they can be seen as a group. In the case of a word containing the 'ough' spelling pattern, they have no need to test phonically each possible sound for that combination of letters, since they know from sight vocabulary, or semantic and syntactic context what the word is. The following sentences contain a number of words with this spelling pattern, and, although the pattern does not always represent the same sound, fluent readers would have no hesitation in reading and understanding the sentences correctly – even though they are rather contrived:

> Because the boy had a cough they thought he ought not to knead the dough.

> Although the weather was rough, we had a drought.

As has been suggested, phonic and sight vocabulary skills for word recognition are best used in combination with context cues. Although context cues may be subdivided into semantic and syntactic cues, it is important to note that semantics are highly dependent upon syntax. Without the structure of syntax there is a severe loss in meaning. For example, if the sentence 'The dog bit the baby' is rearranged so that the normal structure is lost, 'the baby dog the bit', the words remain the same, but the word meanings alone are not sufficient to give the meaning of the string of words. We cannot even be certain whether it is a puppy, or a baby and a dog that is involved. 'Bit' may mean a small part or the past tense of 'bite'. Because of this important role of syntax, the efficient reader is constantly aware of the grammatical structures used in the text, and will predict those structures in the light of past experience of language and knowledge of the author's style.

The following is a transcript of a beginning reader's oral reading of a passage. In brackets are the comments Neil made as he was reading and looking at the pictures. Refer to Appendix 1 (page 87) for a key to the notation used.

'Look, Mum.

This dog followed me.

It will not go home.
<small>c away</small>

Go home.

Go away.'

'Tommy was in bed.
<small>wakes</small>

He did not sleep.

It was hot in the bed.
<small>c I   c not</small>

Then he saw the dog.

The dog looked at Tommy.
<small>up</small>

Then it jumped.

It jumped on to the bed.'
<small>c in</small>

(Is that right?)

(I wonder what she says. Where does she put it?)

(He opens the window to get a bit of breeze and then the dog jumps in. What do you think his Mum'll say? My Mum would say, 'Come on boy.' She'd keep it.)

In this example it is clear that Neil is enjoying the story and is searching for meaning in the text. The substitutions of 'away' for 'home', 'wakes' for 'was', and 'not' for 'hot' all make sense semantically and syntactically. The last miscue is quite a common type of miscue made by beginning readers; early reading texts often try to simplify the reading material by using a short string of words in a sentence, and this often means that a sentence such as 'Then it jumped' is produced. However, as in this case, the beginner is not sufficiently aware of punctuation to anticipate that this is a complete sentence in itself, and he frequently expects the sentence to continue to give more information about where it jumped.

As children learn to read they sometimes pay particular attention to one or two of the word recognition skills at the expense of the others. Whilst to some extent this may be a normal developmental part of learning to read, it may be the cause of reading difficulties for some children. Assessment of the skills being used by children forms the essential basis of diagnostic teaching, leading to the provision of the most suitable instruction and materials for the child.

One useful method of assessing the cues being used by a child is Miscue Analysis, developed by K. S. Goodman (1965). Goodman suggested that by observing the 'miscues' or errors made in oral reading it was possible to gain an insight into the strategies being used by the reader. Goodman suggested that every response was either cued or miscued by the reader's use of one or more strategies in reading a text. The reader samples the graphic display of letters on a page and predicts what the words, syntactic structures and meanings will be. By further sampling, the initial prediction may either be accepted or rejected and the reader may then proceed to make further predictions.

In an article about oral reading miscues, Goodman (1969) lists a taxonomy of 28 cues and miscues. For most purposes, however, it is probably more useful to reduce this to three main areas of cues and miscues: grapho-phonic, semantic and syntactic. Although this makes miscue analysis a more readily usable tool for classroom diagnosis, it is still not simple, since many miscues are caused by combinations of more than one of these cues. For example, in the following extract from a boy's oral reading, he substitutes 'bigger' for 'breaking', 'boy' for 'boat' and 'took' for 'tossed', which would all suggest that he used the grapho-phonic cue of the first letter to predict a word which was syntactically and semantically acceptable within the context of the sentence. However, when he substitutes 'splashed' for 'broke' he was probably paying far less attention to the letters in the word than to the meaning.

There was a boy out on a rock.

The girls got the boat into the sea.

They went over to the rocks.

Waves were‖breaking over the rocks.
(bigger)

They could not pull the boat in.
(boy)

One girl‖tossed a rope to the boy.
(took)

Waves broke over him, but they pulled him to the boat.
(splashed)

There are three main factors influencing the strategies used for word recognition. The first is concerned with the text itself. The choice of text for diagnosis using miscue analysis is very important. Readers do not use a static balance and combination of reading strategies. If a reader finds a text very easy to read, words may be omitted or inserted, or semantically and syntactically acceptable substitutions may be made. This is probably because the reader is more involved with the overall meaning of the text than with the individual words or letters on the page. If, on the other hand, a reader finds a passage difficult to understand, then it is likely that much closer attention will be paid to individual words and letters, and so miscues are more likely to be in the grapho-phonic category.

Secondly, as well as varying with the difficulty or readability of the text, strategies used appear to vary as a developmental part of learning to read. Studies by Biemiller (1970) and Burke (1976) have investigated this. Biemiller's study was of first grade (six-year-old) children and suggested three main phases of development between October and May as they began to learn to read:

(a)   predominant use of contextual cues;
(b)   non-response and graphically constrained miscues;
(c)   increase in the combined use of graphic and contextual cues.

Burke investigated the reading strategies of seven- to nine-year-old children. Using material suitable for the reading skill of the children involved, she found that there was an increase, followed by a decrease, in use of graphic cues. On the other hand, there was an increase, followed by a slight decrease, in the use of syntactic cues. For the use of semantic cues there was shown to be a continuous increase. These results suggest that in the early stages of learning to read, when the child has begun to relate the visual input to the oral form of the words, there is a greater reliance on the visual information than on the semantic acceptability of the responses. As semantic and syntactic cues become more important for the reader less use is made of the visual information. As progress is made the child is better able to make use of all three types of cues.

The third main factor influencing the strategies used by children for word recognition is the teaching method. Barr (1975) and Cohen (1975) both found evidence to support the theory, which in itself has considerable face validity, that children adopt the strategy taught in their schools. If, as seems likely, this theory is indeed true, then this has serious implications for the teaching of reading, since, although children appear to pass through developmental stages in their use of reading strategies, the teaching methods used may be either helping or hindering the development of the use of an integrated system of strategies.

The very fact that it is possible to identify different types of reading skills and strategies might suggest to some that it would be logical to separate these for teaching, concentrating on one at a time. Although this might appear, on the surface, to simplify the teaching and learning of reading, the strategies are so inter-related in the skilled reader that isolating them for beginners may, in fact, cause difficulties by encouraging the forming of habits which may later need to be broken if the reader is to become fully efficient. Contextual cues, phonics and sight vocabulary are all useful tools for the beginning reader as well as the fluent reader, and children should be encouraged to use whichever strategy or combination of strategies is most appropriate for them as they look for meaning in the text.

The efficient use of the strategies described above enables readers to recognise words, correct many of their own miscues, predict the meaning of known and unknown words, make full use of the grammatical structures in a text, and, when necessary, to reproduce the text orally with good intonation. All these basic skills underlie the ability of the reader to understand and make use of a text fully.

In summary, then, word recognition involves not only the ability to reconstruct the oral form of a word, either aloud or subvocally, but also skill in assigning the appropriate meaning to the word within the context of the complete text, the ability to suspend judgment about the meaning of a word or to revise original ideas in the light of succeeding context. It also involves the prediction of words and their meanings from the surrounding context and an understanding of the written conventions of grammar, which often differ from the spoken forms. When called upon to read aloud, the reader needs not only to recognise individual words as a string of separate words to be pronounced, but also to interpret the meaning of the whole in order to reproduce that meaning through the use of intonation.

3 Reading Skills at Paragraph Level

Over sixty years ago E. L. Thorndike (1917) said (page 27): 'Understanding a paragraph is like solving a problem in mathematics. It consists in selecting the right elements of the situation and putting them together in the right relations, and also with the right amount of weight or influence or force for each. The mind is assailed, as it were, by every word in the paragraph. It must select, repress, soften, emphasise, correlate and organise, all under the influence of the right mental set or purpose or demand.'

This statement by Thorndike is still, today, a good summary of what it is thought a reader needs to be able to do in order to understand a paragraph of text adequately. Many check-lists of skills for paragraph or text comprehension have been published since Thorndike wrote this. These are helpful in highlighting the types of thinking and aspects of a text which a reader needs to be able to consider, for example, finding the main idea, understanding relationships of cause and effect, following a sequence; but as Thorndike's last sentence quoted above suggests, different skills and strategies are needed according to the purpose of the reader. It is not sufficient for a child to learn a particular skill; he/she also needs to learn when it is appropriate to use that skill and to apply a learned skill to appropriate reading tasks.

In this section a number of skills needed to read paragraphs or longer texts will be considered. For purposes of discussion it has been necessary to isolate them. In no way, however, is the method of presentation intended to imply that these are discrete skills which can or should be taught in isolation. Indeed, Lunzer and Gardner (1979) concluded from their research that '. . . reading comprehension cannot be broken down into a number of distinct subskills' (page 299). They view reading comprehension not as something the reader does but as a statement about how well the reader's purpose has been achieved. They consider the subskills suggested by other researchers to be different types of comprehension task rather than different kinds of reading, and that the most important factor affecting an individual's comprehension of a text is the ability and the willingness to reflect on its content.

Since it is impossible to observe directly the process of thoughtful reading, it is necessary to look at the behaviours which result from this covert process, and for teachers to promote the appropriate behaviour patterns in their pupils' reading.

In view of the large number of comprehension skills suggested in the literature on the subject (in terms of Lunzer and Gardner's work these might be considered to be comprehension tasks), it may be helpful to subdivide these under the following broad headings based on Barrett's classification (1968):

(a) Literal level;
(b) Inferential level;
(c) Evaluative level;
(d) Appreciative level.

The major elements of these levels are as follows:

(a) *Literal level*
  (i) recognition of explicitly stated facts;
  (ii) recall of explicitly stated facts;
  (iii) sequencing of a story, information or ideas;
  (iv) following straightforward instructions;
  (v) understanding comparisons;
  (vi) understanding straightforward cause and effect relationships.

(b) *Inferential level*
  (i) reorganisation of ideas from the form used by the writer to one more readily used by the reader;
  (ii) reorganisation of linguistic forms to those more readily used by the reader;
  (iii) finding main ideas;
  (iv) finding and understanding ideas not directly stated;
  (v) making predictions in the light of what has been read;
  (vi) interpreting figurative language.

(c) *Evaluative level*
  (i) distinguishing fact from opinion;
  (ii) distinguishing reality from fantasy;
  (iii) judging the validity of a statement;
  (iv) judging the appropriateness of a text to the reader's purpose;
  (v) evaluation of author style, characterisation, and effectiveness of writing;
  (vi) detecting and evaluating author bias.

(d) *Appreciative level*
  This level deals with the reader's affective response to a text. This may include an emotional or aesthetic response to:
  (i) the content of a text;
  (ii) the characters portrayed;
  (iii) the figurative language used.

The 'outcomes of reading' are dependent upon these comprehension skills. A considerable part of the outcomes remains covert and even the reader may not be completely aware of all the outcomes of reading. Included in the outcomes are likely to be the following:

  (i) the learning of new information;
  (ii) the revision of previous ideas and opinions;
  (iii) a change of mood through an affective response;
  (iv) the completion of a task following instructions;
  (v) the ability to answer questions or take part in a discussion on the content, slant or style of writing;
  (vi) the writing of notes.

The measure of success a reader achieves in completing any reading may only be judged in relation to the purpose for reading, since a variety of outcomes from a text may be possible, but only one may be appropriate to the reader's purpose.

As Lunzer and Gardner (1979) concluded, the levels or types of comprehension are not distinct types of reading requiring different reading skills. There would appear to be no straightforward, hierarchical structure linking the levels of comprehension, but they seem to be largely interdependent. To some extent, however, the basis for all other levels of comprehension appears to be the Literal level. Although, at first sight, this appears to be a simple level of comprehension it does, nevertheless, involve complex mental processes in which the words and ideas which are read are matched against previous knowledge and experience in order that the reader may assign meaning to them. Because the past experience of each person is different, every reader reading any one text will have a unique personal view of what it means.

If the literal content of a text is processed by the reader without any further evaluation of its relevance, without links being made with ideas already held in memory, or without any affective response, what is remembered about the text is likely to be at the level of details of information or a general idea of the ideas expressed. It is also likely that readers will find more difficulty in recalling the information than if they had processed the ideas more deeply, for example, by evaluating them in the light of their own past experience.

Alongside the Literal level of comprehension is the Inferential level. This calls for a more active response from the reader, searching for meanings which are not directly stated. It may be that the reader needs to deduce facts or ideas from what is stated; or it may be necessary to interpret figurative language or a linguistic style which is not readily understood. The reader may need to take an overview of a series of ideas in order to discover the main idea the author is trying to communicate.

At this level, the reader also needs to be able to make use of various conventions of the written language, for example, headings and subheadings, or words written in bold print or italics, which all serve to draw attention to a specific point. Certain words and phrases are also commonly used in writing, but not so often in speech, and these serve as signposts for the reader in the search for meaning and the relation of ideas to one another. These include such words and phrases as 'however', 'nevertheless', and 'not only . . . but also . . .'.

Building upon both the Literal and Inferential levels is the Evaluative level. At this level the reader is not only matching ideas read with ideas already stored in memory, but is also considering the author's ideas in the light of previous knowledge and experience, so that some judgment may be made as to whether the new ideas are valid or worth reflecting upon as a means of fulfilling the purpose for reading.

This level of reading is often termed 'Critical Reading' and there is a tendency to feel that this is an advanced reading skill which can best be taught after pupils have learned the basics of reading. However, it is important that evaluation becomes an integral part of reading if readers are to be 'thoughtful readers'. Evaluative reading or critical reading is simply thinking about the content or style of the material being read in relation to the reader's purposes. It is a questioning frame of mind in the reader, who seeks to discover whether what the author says is justified, whether the author has a particular bias, and whether the text is relevant to the purpose the reader has set.

The outcomes leading from this Evaluative level may be either acceptance or rejection of part or all of the author's message, or it may even be the suspending of judgment whilst further research and thinking is undertaken. One outcome is probably a revision of original ideas in the reader's mind (this may be in terms of the material discussed by the author or the reader's opinion of the author), and possibly the addition of new ideas. The outcome may be a physical action involved in doing some task suggested by the text, or a discussion with another person, or taking notes summarising the main ideas. The reader may not be entirely satisfied by using one text and may wish to compare other authors' ideas with the ideas expressed in the first text; or the reader may wish to follow up a particular line of thought or find further information in other texts or sources of information.

In a formal teaching situation it is often difficult for a child to learn to reject a text as being irrelevant to his purposes, since the teacher is usually in the position of setting the purposes, selecting the text, and setting questions which may be answered by reading the text. This can be detrimental to good habits of evaluative reading, since, if children are never expected to decide whether the text is suitable for their needs, they may quickly learn the habit of accepting whatever a passage says unquestioningly, and without thought of comparing two or more different texts on the same subject. It is important that children are given the opportunity and are encouraged to exercise this Evaluative level of reading as early as possible, and this may well be done by encouraging this type of thinking in an oral situation before expecting evaluative thinking in a reading situation.

At the Appreciation level readers are concerned with their emotional response to the material they are reading; for example, do they like the story? How do they feel about the characters portrayed? The affective response may also be found in reading non-fictional material, for example, advertisements, political pamphlets and biographies.

The emotional response may be caused both by the facts or ideas read and by the style of writing used. The use of emotive words is designed to appeal to this emotional response, and is often a sign of prejudice on the part of the writer. Shaw wrote 'When a man wants to murder a tiger, he calls it sport. When a tiger wants to murder him, he calls it ferocity.'

An example of the type of emotive language children may come across, which is designed to produce this affective response, might be found in an advert of this type, probably accompanied by an illustration:

> The fantastic Super-Spider!
> The game you have been waiting for.
> Your friends will be amazed.
> Don't miss your chance to play the game
> that is probably the most exciting ever invented.

4 th

Why it is a 'fantastic' game or people are expected to enjoy playing it
explained. The implication is that having such a game will bring wi.
popularity among friends. Words like 'fantastic', 'amazed', and 'exciting'
build up a feeling about the game. On the other hand, slipping in a word like
'probably' means that no really definite statement of fact is being made.

For the purposes of illustration, this is a rather blatant example; many
writers are more subtle and it is important that pupils should be aware of
their affective response to texts in all types of writing, including fiction and
literature, as well as the more obvious advertising or propaganda. Children
need to be encouraged to develop habits of linking the Appreciative and
Evaluative levels of reading. This will involve them in being aware of their
emotional response to a text and being able to analyse the reasons for this
response. This evaluation will then directly affect the outcome of their
reading, since it may mean either the acceptance or rejection of an author's
ideas and style of presentation.

This type of thinking can be encouraged from the earliest stages of
learning to read by discussing with the children whether they liked or
disliked a story and the characters in it, and asking them to give reasons for
their point of view. In a non-fictional context, primary age children could
undertake a project to investigate the accuracy of claims made by advertisers of a particular commodity of interest to them; through projects of this
type a great deal of thinking and discussion can be encouraged in which the
children need not only to read the words on the page but also to form a
judgment and be able to give valid reasons for having come to a certain
conclusion.

4 Differences between beginning readers and fluent readers

Clearly, if pupils are to be really efficient, thinking readers who can satisfy
whatever need may arise, there is a tremendous amount of learning and
teaching to be done throughout the primary school. Whilst it is important
for the teacher continually to bear in mind the total, efficient reading
process towards which he/she is trying to guide the child, it is also only
realistic to accept that the beginner is unlikely to be able to tackle all aspects
at once.

Perhaps the three main differences between the beginner and the fluent
reader are:

> purpose for reading;
> the size of the units being processed;
> the relationship between reading and oral language.

For the beginner the purpose for reading is very often nothing to do with the content of the text, but simply 'to learn to read'. This can be very helpful if children are well motivated to learn to read, but there is a danger, if they do not quickly discover some value in the content of the texts, that they will become 'unthinking readers', since their main concern will be to get on to the next book in the reading scheme rather than to enjoy a book for its own sake, or to learn something from it.

In the early stages of learning to read children have to pay far more attention to the features of the individual letters making up words than does the fluent reader. This can mean that the child has a problem in holding a sufficient number of items of information in the memory in order to derive the overall meaning of a word, phrase, or sentence. As the child progresses, the recognition of letters and words becomes much faster until it is an automatic process linked with prediction in context. Then, instead of processing the features of individual letters as separate items which need to be remembered in order to build up a total word, phrase or sentence and its meaning, the child is able to process word parts, whole words or even groups of words as if they were a single unit, and the memory is able to cope with longer words and meanings expressed in longer, more involved sentences.

Because silent reading is necessarily a covert process, the beginner is normally taught to read aloud. Whether children need to read aloud to translate the written form of the language into the oral form they are used to hearing in order to understand the meaning of the text, has not been fully investigated. It may be that they seem to need to hear the words before they understand them because of the way they have been taught. Whichever of these may be the case for the beginner, our society expects people to read silently unless they have a specific reason for reading aloud, and most children seem to have little difficulty in transferring to reading silently after the initial stages of reading instruction. However, many children do continue to make the relevant lip movements for some time, suggesting that they are subvocalising the words. Nevertheless, it is still impossible to say from this that they can derive the meaning of the text only via the oral form of the language, since this may just be a habit of reading aloud that has not entirely disappeared.

Perhaps one of the most noticeable differences between the oral reading of the beginner and that of the efficient reader is that the beginner reads words aloud before understanding the total meaning of the phrase or sentence, whereas the efficient reader has already understood the text before pronouncing the words. This enables the efficient reader to give the correct intonation and stress patterns to the words to recreate the meaning of the text for the listener. This does not exclude the possibility that young children may also be efficient readers in the context of some familiar material, which they are able to read for the benefit of their listeners as well as themselves.

2 Classifying reading comprehension tasks

The words 'Comprehension Exercises' will, for many, immediately bring to mind the traditional passage to be read, followed by a number of questions to be answered from the passage. The value of this type of exercise will be discussed in Chapter 5. However, there are many different kinds of exercise or reading activity which can also be used to promote reading comprehension. Many teachers have devised their own activities or extended or adapted others which are of more value for the children they are teaching. A selection from the many possible kinds of activity is described below (Chapter 5). It is intended at this point to outline the main demands made on the child by the reading material and the way in which the child, as reader, needs to make use of that material. This broad classification of reading tasks is intended to serve as a guide to the teacher in planning the reading curriculum, so that as many different types of reading activity as are possible and appropriate for each child can be introduced to the programme of reading instruction.

There are a number of different approaches to such a classification; four will be discussed in this chapter:

> the purpose of the reader;
> the type of reading material being used;
> the purpose of the author;
> the skills and techniques needed by the reader.

A reading task cannot be considered in terms of just one of these dimensions, but must take into account all four. By considering the ways in which comprehension tasks may be classified it is hoped that teachers will be alerted to the great diversity of the reading tasks which children need to be able to deal with, and that they may be enabled to help children to do this flexibly, effectively, and thoughtfully from the early stages of learning to read.

The importance of 'purpose' in reading has already been discussed, and one of the most basic ways of classifying a reading task is by the purpose the reader sees in the task. It may be that the child considers that the task has:

(a) an intrinsic purpose;

(b) no intrinsic purpose except one of improving reading skills;

(c) no purpose.

Within section (a) Merritt (1974) has suggested five areas in which human purposes are exercised:

(i) home and family;

(ii) leisure;

(iii) consumer;

(iv) community;

(v) employment.

In the home and family section are included such things as reading a recipe or a car maintenance manual. Leisure might include reading a novel or instructions for a particular hobby or game. As a consumer the reader is concerned with reading advertisements or reports on articles he may wish to buy. In the area of community the reader may need to read notices or reports of local events. At work a reader may need to read a variety of notices, instructions and other documents in order to carry out a job effectively.

Moyle (1976) has suggested a second way of classifying reading tasks by the type of reading material to be used. This includes a wide range of different types of reading materials, different author purposes, and different styles of writing. The following list, although not a complete one, illustrates the range of materials which could be used in the classroom:

fiction;
textbooks;
reference books;
magazines;
newspapers;
comics;
brochures;
leaflets;
advertisements;
notices;
forms and questionnaires;
instructions;
letters;
children's own written work of a variety of types.

Reading materials may also be classified according to the purpose of the author. The main types of author purpose identified by Moyle are as follows:

to entertain;
to inform;
to instruct;
to persuade;
to question;
to command.

These author purposes are not discrete, and almost any type of written material may have a combination of author purposes, although one purpose may be stronger than the other subsidiary purposes. If children are to be able to think about the material they read as effectively as possible, they need to learn to be aware of the purpose of the author.

Frequently linked with the author's purpose is the style of writing which might be described by one or more of the following headings (and there may be other styles not identified here):

descriptive;
persuasive;
imperative;
interrogative;
declamatory.

It is important that children should be given the opportunity to meet a variety of writing styles as they learn to read, so that they can be aware of the effect the author is trying to make upon their thinking by the use of a particular style of writing. This should enable them to make the most appropriate choice of reading material in relation to their own particular reading purposes, and to read that material with more insight.

Finally, reading activities may be classified according to the skills and techniques needed in order to read effectively. Merritt (1973) has divided these skills and techniques into the following groups:

Goal Setting skills;
Planning skills;
Reading skills (Implementation);
Development skills.

This grouping of skills is in accordance with the sequence in which the skills would normally be used to carry out a reading task. Firstly, in Goal Setting skills the general purposes and specific questions to be answered by reading are decided. Then at the Planning stage the readers use those skills which enable them to locate suitable material, evaluate its potential usefulness, and decide on the most suitable strategies to be used in reading in order to answer the questions previously set. Reading or Implementation skills include those of word attack, linguistic knowledge, and comprehension skills. At the fourth stage, Development skills involve the reader in evaluating the usefulness of the material read and the appropriateness of the strategies used; they also include deciding on any action that should be taken as a result of the reading: this may include deciding on a way of storing or communicating information.

In any reading activity all four areas of reader's purpose, media, author's purpose and skills and techniques will be involved, and each must be considered; however, the emphasis for teaching and learning will probably lie in the one area which the teacher had in mind as the activity was planned. If the emphasis lies in skills and techniques, then care must be taken that the pupil not only learns those skills and techniques, but also learns when and how to apply them in other reading situations. It is also important that the children learn to use the full range of skills and techniques at the appropriate stage in their development.

If children are to read independently and effectively they must also be able to cope with the wide range of reading material that they are likely to come into contact with. It is very easy for books alone to become the major source of reading material in schools, supplemented by worksheets or other teacher produced material, and this implies that these two categories are the only materials the children should read, whereas in actual fact these are only a small selection of the total reading material available. Unless children are encouraged to use a wide range of materials, they are being given a very narrow view of reading and are losing an opportunity to learn to appreciate and criticise a range of media, styles of writing, and author purposes.

There are a number of advantages to be gained by beginning to plan a reading activity from the point of view of the reader's purpose. Moyle (1976, page 222) lists the advantages as follows:

> Motivates the child to read with some specific end in mind.
> Sets the type of reading behaviour which is most appropriate to the task.
> Sets the questions to which answers are to be found and helps the reader ensure that suitable materials are selected.
> Relates the work to living in general and enables the child to transfer skill learning from one task to similar tasks.

Whilst all these reasons are important, perhaps the major one is the last one listed. Transfer of learning seems to be a problem for many children. Most teachers will have observed children who, having been taught a particular phonic rule, can use that rule when directed, but seem unable to apply the rule for themselves unless they are told to do so. Similarly, children can be taught how to use an index and may be able to explain the purpose and use of an index quite satisfactorily, but in a practical situation, without guidance, seem to be unaware of the appropriate use of the skill they have learned. If children are taught skills 'in context', there would seem to be a better chance that they will also learn when it is appropriate to use that skill.

The wide range of purposes, media and skills listed above poses the question for the teacher: when should teaching of the total reading curriculum begin? The answer is probably 'at the pre-reading stage'. Even before children begin to learn to read, the foundations for 'thoughtful reading' are built, as the children learn to investigate and think about the world around them, as they learn to communicate through oral language, and as they learn to listen to stories read to them. 'Thoughtful reading' involves thinking about a message communicated through a visual code system; children can begin to learn how to think about a message communicated through an aural code as a basis on which to build thoughtful reading. C. M. McCullough (1957) tested first grade children (six-year-olds) on their comprehension of main idea, details, sequence and creative reading. She found (page 66) that:

> It is clear, at least in the case of these children, that the group is capable of answering the different types of items about story material even before learning to read. It should be admitted that children can be trained to think only in terms of the facts of a story if the teacher asks them only facts . . .

Learning to think has begun long before children enter school and this should be continued as part of learning to read.

The introduction of the many and varied types of reading materials and occasions will depend upon the readiness of the child. In 'reading readiness' for the very beginnings of learning to read, a child needs to have reached an appropriate level of visual and auditory perception, oral language usage and attention control, to have a wide range of experiences and an interest in and understanding of the use of written material, and to be well motivated to learn to read. Similarly, a pupil needs to be 'ready' to learn a new skill or to approach a new type of written material. As with 'reading readiness' for the complete beginner, the 'readiness' for each stage of development is difficult to define precisely. There also seems to be no strict sequential order in which the learning should take place. It is likely that the most important factor in this 'readiness' is whether or not children see a purpose in what they are learning and are well motivated. If children have begun a reading task with a purpose they can accept and identify with, they will be better able to see the need for the new learning and will be able to learn when as well as how to use the new skill.

The teacher who sets out to plan a reading activity from the starting point of the reader's purpose, must be aware of the skills and resources a child will need to carry out a particular task, and should be ready to intervene with the appropriate help, support, or instruction, which will enable the child not only to complete a specific task, but also to further his/her reading development. There is clearly a great deal involved in this complex task for both child and teacher. One way in which Moyle has suggested the teacher can organise reading instruction of this type is to draw up a matrix of questions, sources of information, types of reference materials and skills, which may be used to complete a reading activity. This acts as an aid to the teacher to ensure that as wide a range of resources and skills as is appropriate is being used. The teacher may also predict with some accuracy the areas for teaching which will be needed by certain children or groups of children. Planning of this type, coupled with the Goals, Planning, Implementation and Development (GPID) skills that the children are encouraged to use, helps to provide a definite structure to the learning task. Information about the children's progress and ability to work effectively on these tasks may be gained by observation of them as they work and the difficulties they encounter; these observations can then form the basis of a record of each child's development in learning to use reading.

The following example of the matrix outlined above might be used by children of about nine years of age.

Purpose

To find out about the Fire Brigade.

Questions	Sources	References	Skills
What equipment do firemen use?	Local Fire Station	Interviews	Transposing spoken language into written language
	Library	Reference books	Indexing Interpreting diagrams Scanning Synthesising.
What happens at a house fire?	Fire Brigade Library	Newspapers Interviews Reference Books Poetry	Evaluating different points of view Considering effect of styles of writing Understanding technical language.

Questions	Sources	References	Skills
How were fires fought in the past?	Museum Library	Exhibits of old equipment. Text Books Reference Books Fiction	Collecting and organising information. Indexing, scanning, skimming, summarising. Comparing, evaluating, synthesising.
How can fires be prevented?	Fire Brigade RoSPA*	Interviews Posters	Transposing oral languaging into written language. Summarising. Interpreting diagrams.

This example is by no means exhaustive of all the possible questions, sources, references, and skills that could be used to achieve the purpose of finding out about the Fire Brigade, but it does serve to show how the use of a matrix of this type can aid both the pupil and the teacher in clarifying exactly what is to be studied, and which materials and resources, skills and techniques will be needed to carry out the task. By the use of this type of matrix, the teacher can check that a wide range of media is being used and that the most appropriate sources of information are made available for the children's use. Because the learning situation is structured in this way, it is more likely that the situation can be avoided in which the child, over-whelmed by the complexity of the task, copies long passages from the first book found to have any relevant information in it. It also makes it possible for the teacher to judge at which stage in the child's work it may be necessary to intervene with support, direct instruction, or advice, in order that the child may complete the task satisfactorily, and most efficiently exercise previously learned or new skills.

*Royal Society for the Prevention of Accidents

3 Characteristics of the 'thoughtful reader'

Some years ago a good reader might have been defined as a reader who performed well on a sight word reading test. In recent years the emphasis has shifted from the 'mechanics' of reading to the ability to use reading and thinking skills in a flexible, efficient, and appropriate way. Reading involves the whole person rather than just the ability to relate the written form of a word to the oral form. In attempting to help children to become 'thoughtful readers' it is, perhaps, helpful to consider the characteristics of people, which seem to be related to their ability and willingness to read thoughtfully.

The following seven characteristics and needs of 'thoughtful readers' have been selected for discussion in this chapter since they seem to have a direct relationship to a reader's thoughtfulness and effectiveness:

(1) good motivation;
(2) a good self-concept;
(3) an understanding of the ideas in the text;
(4) an understanding of the language of the text;
(5) an appropriate attitude;
(6) effective use of appropriate reading strategies;
(7) the need for thought-provoking reading materials and the ability to select appropriate material.

As our knowledge in this important area in the field of teaching reading increases, it may well be found that this list is incomplete or that some of these areas are of far less importance than others. However, it is hoped that they may form a basis for diagnosing children's needs and that they may be of some guidance in planning reading instruction.

1 The 'thoughtful reader' is well-motivated

It is natural for people to take more trouble and care over doing something in which they can see a definite value than over something which appears to them to be of little or no value. This is true of human behaviour in general and includes reading behaviour. This appreciation of the value of a task and the resulting effect this has upon the effort made to complete the task is commonly referred to as 'motivation'.

There are two main types of motivation: internal and external. With internal motivation the person is able to see some intrinsic value in the task itself. In terms of reading this might be a child who is reading a reference book on dinosaurs in order to plan a model, or a novel for the enjoyment gained from it. The reader has a clear purpose for reading.

External motivation is the appreciation of a reason outside the task itself for completing the task. External motivation for reading might be the desire to receive praise and attention from a teacher, or perhaps the need to find out specific information in order to complete an assignment set by a teacher – the pupil being relatively uninterested in the content of the assignment.

Both internal and external motivation are used by teachers. This may be a deliberate policy or it may happen unintentionally. However, since motivation would appear to have an effect on the quality of the effort the reader makes, it must be taken into account for the most effective learning to be able to take place. Although both internal and external motivation may appropriately be used in the classroom, the most helpful attitudes towards reading are likely to be fostered by the use of internal motivation. Internal motivation is more likely to produce independent readers who are ready and able to use their reading skills when they are away from the teacher's support and encouragement.

As was stated above, good motivation produces greater effort on the part of the reader, and this is seen in increased attention and perseverance with a reading task. The attention and perseverance manifested by well-motivated readers can frequently enable them to read material which would normally be considered to be too difficult for them. Conversely, if children have little interest in the material they are reading, they will make less effort to read and think about it.

Because of the influence motivation can have on progress in learning to read and the development of helpful attitudes towards reading, it is important that the interests of children are taken into account when materials for teaching reading are being selected for a child. It is clearly not sufficient to select a reading book from a reading scheme on the basis of reading age alone; the interests of each individual must also be taken into account. A variety of different reading schemes and other materials are likely to be needed by a class of children who will have different interests, likes, and dislikes. Discussions with individuals and groups can help the teacher to select suitable reading materials for individuals and also encourage children to try something new.

2 The 'thoughtful reader' has a good self-concept

A good self-concept is an important characteristic of a thoughtful reader. Confidence in one's ability to perform a task removes most of the stress and worry which could hinder the actual completion of that task. If children are under stress because they fear they will be unable to succeed in completing a reading activity, then their attention is likely to be diverted from that activity to worries about what may happen if they fail; because attention is diminished, the children are then more likely to fail or produce less than their best performance. Thus, a poor self-concept may become a self-fulfilling prophecy. As Smith (1978, page 10) says:

'Anxiety about being able to comprehend and remember can make any reader functionally blind.'

In the more specific area of critical or evaluative reading, the task requires readers to have a good measure of confidence in their own ability to consider and evaluate material that is read. It is all too easy for a reader to think, because something has been printed and published, that it must, therefore, be true. A good self-concept and confidence in one's own ability to evaluate ideas to form an opinion, which one can substantiate by reference to various valid sources, is important if children are to be able to learn to read with an open and independent mind.

3 The 'thoughtful reader' understands the ideas in the text

I wish to present some of our results pertaining to laminar lesions caused by monoenergetic heavy particles in the cerebral cortex of the rabbit.

Rose, Malis, Baker (1961, page 22)

It is not suggested that material of the type quoted here is appropriate for use in a primary school classroom. It has been deliberately chosen for inclusion in order to illustrate to the fluent adult reader the difficulties that children face in materials for which they are inadequately prepared.

Without some background understanding of the structure of the brain and of radiation, it is impossible to have any real understanding of this opening sentence of a research report. In a similar way, children may be confronted by textbooks, reference books, or fiction which appear equally unintelligible to them, not because the text is wrong, nor because the child is not making an effort to understand, but rather because the background knowledge, which is vital for an understanding of the text, is lacking.

Comprehension involves the relating of ideas read in the text to ideas already known and integrated into the individual's picture and understanding of the world. This individual theory of the world, or cognitive structure, is constantly being adapted to incorporate new or changed ideas and concepts. These new ideas or concepts can, however, only usefully be integrated into an existing schema of related concepts. It is, perhaps, helpful to consider the mind as containing some kind of network linking all the related ideas and items stored within it; the more links that can be forged, and the more ideas and items of information that can be incorporated into the system, the richer and more useful can that system become.

4 The 'thoughtful reader' understands the language in which the text is written

It seems a rather obvious statement to say that a reader needs to be able to understand the language of the text in order to be able to understand the message conveyed by that text.

Als U deze zin kunt verstaan, kunt U waarschijnlijk ook het Nederlands spreken.

Most readers of this monograph are unlikely to be able to understand this sentence; translated into English it is: If you can understand this sentence you can probably speak Dutch too. In the Dutch sentence the vocabulary is totally meaningless for most people; but if the words are familiar, as in the English translation, then the meaning is clear. A similar situation can arise in the vernacular language if vocabulary is unfamiliar to the reader. However, it is important to distinguish between difficulties caused by unfamiliar vocabulary and difficulties caused by unfamiliar ideas which are also expressed in unfamiliar vocabulary; if the problem is solely one of vocabulary, then it may be solved by substituting a synonym, but if the problem is caused by a lack of understanding of the concept as well as the word then further explanation and help will be needed.

A reader needs not only to be aware of the most common meaning of a word, but also of its other meanings and connotations; for example, the apparently simple word 'black' has among its many meanings the following: the opposite of white, dark-skinned, gloomy, dirty, sinister, wicked, funereal, and to exclude; and that is without including phrases such as: black and blue, or putting something down in black and white. Clearly a broad understanding of vocabulary is vital for comprehension of a text. Downing (1970) has also drawn attention to the importance for the child of a sound understanding of the abstract vocabulary used to talk about reading during reading instruction. In his research he found that children had particular difficulty in understanding terms such as 'sound', and 'word', which are so commonly used. It is probable that many children who have difficulty in learning to read are still confused about the meanings of these terms, and until the confusion is resolved any remedial teaching involving the use of these terms will be of only limited benefit to them. It may also be that, had they been carefully taught the meanings of these terms at an appropriate level in their development, many of their difficulties could have been more easily overcome, or might never have arisen at all.

Grammatical structures in written language are frequently very different from those used in spoken language. Written structures are often more complex. The comprehending reader needs to be able to deal with the various grammatical structures met with in a text. At a simple level a reader needs to understand the meaning conveyed by the word order of sentences such as: 'The dog bit the man' and 'The man bit the dog.' (This is equally true of oral and written language.)

At a more complex level, the reader needs to be able to understand the relationships between ideas within a sentence and between sentences. The following example has been selected to illustrate some of the common problems involved in understanding meaning conveyed by grammatical structure; it is not intended to be illustrative of the type of material commonly read by young children, although they will meet similar structures in many textbooks, nor is it suggested that these are the only structures which may cause difficulties.

In fact, quite apart from whatever intrinsic value they may possess, many educational innovations and movements of the past three decades – activity programmes, project and discussion methods, various ways of maximising non-verbal and manipulative experience in the classroom, emphasis on 'self-discovery' and on learning for and by *problem-solving* – owe their origins and popularity to widespread dissatisfaction with the techniques of verbal instruction.

Ausubel (1963, page 193)

Perhaps the first impression on reading this sentence is that the sentence structure used helps to make the point about the difficulties of verbal instruction. The very length of the sentence makes it difficult to cope with, since many elements need to be held in mind right through to the end in order to grasp their relationship with one another. The skilled reader is able to recognise the section in parentheses and know that this is simply qualifying the previous phrase, 'many educational innovations and movements of the past three decades'; knowing this they are able to concentrate on the main part of the sentence: '. . . many educational innovations and movements of the past three decades . . . owe their origins and popularity to widespread dissatisfaction with the techniques of verbal instruction.' In this sentence there are also examples of anaphoric and cataphoric references (words which refer to a previous statement or to later elements of the text). The first two words, 'in fact', refer back to the previous sentence and suggest a qualification of the previous statement. The pronoun 'they', in the clause 'whatever intrinsic value *they* may possess', refers to the later section of the sentence: 'many educational innovations and movements of the last three decades'. It would be possible to analyse this sentence in greater depth and to give other examples of sentence structures which can prove difficult for the reader to understand, but this brief example suffices to show that children need to be prepared to meet and cope with these difficulties; it is not sufficient to assume that because the words can be read and the meanings of individual words are known, that the reader will also understand the total meaning of a sentence or passage.

Certain phrases or expressions can be a source of particular difficulty to the young reader. Reading the sentence, 'The boy was anything but happy', many children, who could pronounce all the words correctly and read the sentence with suitable intonation, if questioned about the meaning, would reveal that they believed that the boy *was* happy. They would be familiar with all the words, but the meaning of a specific combination of those words would not be understood. These structures or phrases, which are less common in the spoken language, need to be carefully introduced to the young reader, and a check needs to be made that the child has fully understood the meaning conveyed by the grammatical structure. Other structures causing similar difficulties for children have been noted by Reid (1972).

It is important that schools make it a part of their curriculum policy to extend the vocabulary of their pupils; however, it would be an impossible objective for teachers to try to teach the meanings of all the words each individual is likely to meet both at school and in adult life. It is, therefore, necessary for pupils to learn how to cope with unfamiliar vocabulary independently. There are three main ways in which a reader can discover the meaning of a word, and these may be used in combination:

(a) use of context;
(b) use of a dictionary;
(c) word analysis.

(a) use of context
The surrounding context of a word can often give many clues to its meaning, and these clues can be both semantic and syntactic, for example, if a reader meets an unknown word such as 'zoyte' in the sentence, 'Jane hit the zoyte and it ran off whimpering', it is fairly safe to guess that the word

'zoyte' refers to an animal that dislikes being hit but is unlikely to retaliate; although this is a guess it is an informed guess and a reasonable supposition in terms of the context. However, as in this case, context can leave a level of uncertainty as to the precise meaning of a word. In such a case dictionary skills might be used.

(b) use of a dictionary

Skill in using a dictionary involves finding a word according to alphabetical order and then selecting the appropriate meaning for the specific context. Many children are able to find a word in a dictionary, but then tend to take the first meaning given or are confused because there are a number of alternatives to choose from, for example, they may need to look up the word 'sole'; unless they are aware of the need to look beyond the first definition they may be very confused by trying to relate the definition of 'sole' as the underneath of a foot to the sentence 'The fisherman caught a fine sole.' Specific instruction needs to be given in selecting the appropriate meaning for the context in which the word is found.

(c) word analysis

An understanding of the use and function of prefixes and suffixes can also help to clarify the meaning of a word. It cannot be assumed that all children automatically learn the meanings of affixes such as un-, dis-, -less, and -ly. Skill in analysing the parts of unknown words can often yield clues to the meanings of those words, for example if children who know the meanings of words such as 'important', 'kind', 'tidy' and other similar adjectives, are taught the meaning of the prefix 'un-', then they will probably also be able to comprehend many of the adjectives formed with this prefix.

Any one of these three skills, use of context, use of a dictionary, and word analysis, is not in itself sufficient for the most efficient and independent reader. All these skills need to be mastered and used in combination with each other.

5 The 'thoughtful reader' has appropriate attitudes to reading

All thoughtful readers must be able to approach each reading occasion with appropriate attitudes. They must have a sound idea of why they are going to read a particular text and what they hope to achieve by that reading. Their purpose may be to find a specific piece of information, to gain enjoyment, or to sample a text to decide whether it is suitable for their needs, but unless they have a definite, purposeful attitude towards reading that text, they will be unlikely to focus their attention on it in the most effective way.

6 The 'thoughtful reader' is able to make effective use of appropriate reading strategies

Linked with the reader's attitudes and purposes for reading are the strategies used. Effective readers need to be able to use the skills of skimming, scanning and study reading and, in addition, to be able to select and use the appropriate reading strategy to fulfill their purpose on any occasion. If children are only provided with instruction in study reading, they may never learn to use the other strategies. If, on the other hand, they are habitually asked to read to find specific items of information in a text, then they may never learn to read for a general impression and overview of a piece of writing. 'Thoughtful readers' have a repertoire of reading strategies, which they can call upon as the situation demands, rather than using only one or two of these strategies from force of habit.

7 The 'thoughtful reader' needs thought-provoking reading materials

Perhaps it may sound obvious that thoughtful readers need to have material to read which they consider is worth thinking about. Within the context of the primary school this means that great care must be taken in the choice of material for reading instruction. These materials are normally selected by the teacher and a number of factors need to be considered before a child is given a book or a worksheet:

(a) *Does the material make sense to the child?*
Particularly at the earliest stages, some reading schemes may not make sense in the mind of the child; the language is distorted in an attempt to restrict and repeat vocabulary, producing some very unnatural texts.

(b) *Is the content of the text thought-provoking?*
Unless there is something in a text which is likely to stimulate the child to think about its content there is little encouragement or scope for practice in becoming a 'thoughtful reader'.

(c) *Is the content of the text suited to the interests of the child?*
Children may be introduced to new ideas and interests, but they may also be discouraged from reading if they find no interest in the materials they are given to read.

(d) *Is the text of a suitable readability level for the child, taking into account the purpose for which it is to be used?*
There is nothing sacrosanct about matching a child's reading age with the

readability level of the material read (difficulties in accurately measuring reading ages and readability levels make this almost impossible in any case); often children enjoy reading 'easy' material and gain great benefit from this, since it frees them to think about the content and really enjoy the text. On the other hand, if children particularly want to try a text which the teacher considers is probably a little difficult for them, with support they are also likely to benefit from this. However, if children are having to pay considerable attention to individual words, they may be unable to give attention to the total meaning of a passage, sentence, or even a phrase.

(e) Can the child select appropriate material?

At the independent level, 'thoughtful readers' are able to select suitable materials to meet their own purposes, have a good knowledge of the types of material available to them, where they can be located, and how they can best be used for a specific purpose.

4 The influence of the teacher

For the majority of children, the first formal teaching of reading is received in the primary school. In these early stages it is vital that helpful attitudes, strategies and habits are encouraged, so that, at a later stage, time does not need to be spent 'unlearning' one habit before a more appropriate one can be learned. Many attitudes and habits are taught and learned unintentionally and teachers need to be aware of the implications of what they do and say, as well as of their immediate teaching objectives.

Choosing a teaching method

The implications of a teaching method need to be considered most carefully when one particular method for teaching reading is to be used. To take an extreme example, if the method chosen is predominantly phonic, this may leave the child with the impression that reading is sounding letters, that it is important to look at every letter of every word and that all words can be recognised by a phonic strategy. Whilst it is unrealistic to expect the child, who is just beginning to learn to read, to understand and know all about the nature and process of reading, it is also unhelpful to teach in such a way that misapprehensions and misunderstandings are fostered.

A similar situation can also occur in teaching 'remedial readers'. In an attempt to rationalise a remedial reading programme, there is a danger of overemphasising one aspect of the reading process, for example, phonics, as discussed above, and teaching this in isolation. By so doing, the teacher may succeed in teaching that one aspect of the reading process, but, by isolating that one part, may hinder the child from learning to integrate the many necessary strategies for effective reading. In addition, by concentrating on the reading process, it may be that the child will lose sight of the essential meaning-getting purpose of reading.

If the teacher emphasises 'getting the words right' so will the children. If the teacher discusses the meaning of the text with the children, they are more likely to look for meaning and think about the content of what they read.

Children can be trained to be thinking readers at any level.

Stauffer (1977, page 246)

It is the frame of mind to think about the information in a page of print that teachers need to encourage (and this, of course, involves adequate accuracy in reading); unless children learn that this is what teachers expect of them, they may not automatically become thoughtful readers.

Fostering appropriate attitudes towards reading

Teachers have a great responsibility in setting the tone of the learning situation and fostering helpful attitudes. Much of this is not directly taught but is present in what has come to be termed 'the hidden curriculum'. In the relatively simple field of choosing and displaying reading materials for the classroom, the general appearance of the materials can give a child an impression of their value; dog-eared, dirty, torn pages are unlikely to suggest to the child that reading is an attractive and valued activity. A reading scheme which is totally separate from other reading materials may suggest that there are two kinds of reading. Materials which have little interest for the children may teach them that reading is uninteresting. Solely fictional material may give children a very limited outlook on reading. Materials which are too difficult may produce a stressful situation. The list could go on with other examples illustrating the need for great care and sympathetic understanding of the children in any choice and display of reading materials.

Similarly the choice of reading activities can also give a false impression of what reading is. The importance of purpose was discussed above, and it must be stressed that an activity should have purpose in the eyes of the child. Without this, not only will motivation be decreased, but the child may come to the conclusion that reading has no purpose. At another level the children need to have experience of a wide range of purposeful activities or they may derive a very limited view of the purpose of reading.

Effects of expectations of progress on pupils' performances

During the last few years there has been some argument about whether or not a teacher's expectations of a child's performance do in fact have an effect on that performance and become a self-fulfilling prophecy. Rosenthal and Jacobson's (1968) research was not entirely conclusive, perhaps because of the ethical difficulties of research in this area (Pidgeon's 1970 book is also relevant here). However, Rosenthal and Jacobson concluded that teachers' expectations of pupils affected their treatment of pupils and so contributed to the formation of pupils' self-concepts, expectations of their own behaviour, motivation and cognitive style and skills. It seems that teachers will set more demanding work for children who are believed to be capable of a high level of achievement, and others, who may be of equal potential, may not be given the opportunity to develop to their full potential. Children may detect their teachers' expectations of them and this may affect the effort they put into a task. In spite of the fact that this theory has not been proved conclusively, and there is a danger that it may be true, teachers should take steps to avoid causing pupils to become under-achievers in this way.

Perhaps it is important, at this point, to distinguish between expectations and hopes or wishes; an expectation is an evaluation, conscious or unconscious, of another person or oneself. This evaluation leads to the person being treated as if the assessment of ability or potential were correct. If one hopes a child will achieve a certain level, one is still aware that this may not be possible; if the expectation is that the child will achieve that level, then there is much less uncertainty in the mind of the assessor.

The teacher is, however, by no means the only source of expectations for the child; probably the most important of the others are parents and peers. In the field of reading both parents and peers will often show their expectations for the child by their reactions to a book being read. The well-meaning comment, in a particular tone of voice, such as 'He's tried hard' or 'She's doing quite well' may only serve to reinforce the idea in the children's minds that they are unlikely ever to read well.

Finn (1972, page 130) quotes the results of one piece of research into the effects of children's own expectations for failure:

> In a cognitive framework, Kagan and Moss (1962) report correlations of the order of $+.70$ between children's expectations for failure in problem situations, and withdrawal from the situation.

It would seem likely that a similarly high correlation might be found in the context of learning to read. Clearly, children must be given confidence in their own ability to succeed, not only by what teachers say, but also through the type of work they set, the materials they use and their general attitude to the learning situation.

Effects of stress on learning

Stress is another factor which may adversely affect progress in learning to read, and may be connected with expectations of teachers, parents, and peers. A rather simplified view of the situation which may arise, is that readers may become so concerned about a possible failure, and may be so worried about the possible consequences of this, that they are unable to pay sufficient attention to the task to enable them to complete it successfully, or they may withdraw from the situation rather than risk an attempt which may fail.

Bruner (1973) suggests that stress makes generic coding of learning less likely and that stress also seems to affect the ability to use already acquired coding systems to go beyond the information given. Thus, in a stressful learning situation, the child may not only be unable to learn new skills and information effectively for future use in a new situation, but may also be unable to use and apply previously learned skills and information, in a different context. Since it is the aim of teachers to provide children with the skills and knowledge needed to use their reading independently, stress, arising from any one of a number of sources, including the teacher and the home, needs to be removed for the most effective learning to be possible.

Fostering independence in reading to learn

Learning to read may be described as learning to receive a message communicated through a written code and to interpret and evaluate that message. Reading to learn is the use individuals are able to make of their reading skills in order to satisfy particular needs. There is a danger of assuming that, because children have a reading age equivalent to or above their chronological age, they can also use their reading to learn. Children may even be very 'thoughtful readers' in relation to material presented to them by the teacher, but be unable or inefficient in finding material to answer their own purposes. In an unpublished study (Wilson, 1977) the author found that a group of nine- and ten-year-olds, who all had reading ages which were higher than their chronological ages, had a knowledge of the skills they needed to locate the information texts they required, but were unable to use those skills efficiently. Whilst it is not possible to generalise from the small sample used in this study, it would appear to be necessary to bridge the gap between 'learning to read' and 'reading to learn' not simply by teaching about reading skills but by giving children adequate opportunity to use those skills in a practical and, as near as possible, a realistic situation. Perhaps there are four main areas which need to be included in a teaching programme to cater for this:

(1) the opportunity for children to learn to set their own purposes for reading;
(2) learning to locate suitable materials, information within a text and evaluating its relevance and usefulness;
(3) learning to use a number of texts or sources and comparing or synthesising findings;
(4) learning to make appropriate use of the information that is found.

Classroom organisation

The reading environment in the classroom is another factor influencing the effectiveness of the teaching of reading. Only a brief outline of the major influences of this can be included here; but since it requires a great deal of thought and effort on the part of the teacher, an enthusiastic teacher is probably the key to the whole situation. The enthusiastic teacher would be well-motivated to explore the many possible methods, approaches, and materials available for use and to make an informed choice from among them.

Whatever the materials available for reading activities in the classroom, they need to be stored or displayed in such a way that both teacher and child are able to find the material they need with the maximum of efficiency. It is surprising how much teaching time can be lost by poorly thought out or inadequately kept storage systems; it is also likely that enthusiasm for an activity will be diminished if the required materials cannot be found relatively easily. The precise form of this organisation must necessarily depend upon the constraints of the classroom, the skills and abilities of the children, and the teaching style adopted by the teacher.

It may sound obvious that, before deciding what to teach and how to teach it, it is first necessary to ascertain just what the child needs to be taught; this is commonly termed 'diagnosis' and it is very important for the most effective teaching, since without this diagnosis a teacher may be teaching something a child already knows, or trying to teach something for which the child is not yet ready.

Diagnosing children's needs

The way in which a teacher decides to undertake the diagnosis of pupil needs is an individual matter, affected by many factors such as class size, materials available, policies instituted by the school and the teacher's own philosophy of teaching reading. Detailed records may be passed from the previous teacher, or, as children move from one class to another, assessment of their needs may have to be begun afresh. Whatever methods are employed, it is important that the results are used; it is a waste of teaching time to spend time diagnosing a child's needs and difficulties, if the results are not to be used as the basis for planning a teaching programme. It is also important that the diagnosis is an ongoing system of working, so that after diagnosis and teaching there is a further assessment of whether or not the child has learned what was taught and what the next stage for teaching should be. The following flow chart illustrates this teaching strategy:

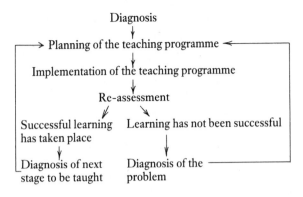

From the point of view of a busy classroom teacher, individual diagnosis can be a daunting task. Published diagnostic tests can be used, but it is probably more helpful to use the child's responses in the normal classroom activities as a basis for assessment. Record keeping of the relevant information can be very time consuming. Individual teachers need to decide whether they will find anecdotal notes, check-lists, or some other system most useful. If a check-list system is used, a five-point scale indicating the child's degree of mastery on each item would be more informative than just a 'yes/no', since in many cases teachers may wish to indicate that a child has learned something but that there is still room for improvement. The date of each assessment also needs to be noted, so that a child's development can be monitored over a year or more. Ideally a check-list should be drawn up by the individual teacher with a group of pupils in mind. The check-lists in Appendix 2 are merely examples of the types of items which teachers may find useful in diagnosing the needs of children at three broad stages in learning to read. Four important areas which may usefully be observed have been covered in them:

attitudes;
intellectual skills;
work habits;
physical well-being.

The importance of appropriate attitudes towards reading has already been discussed and can best be assessed by observation of children as well as talking to them about reading and the books they read. Intellectual skills cover those aspects of reading such as communication skills, memory and sequencing, word recognition and finding and using an appropriate text effectively. Work habits include the ability to attend to a speaker or a text, working relationships with others and the ability to concentrate on a task and complete it. It may be that some children need help in controlling their attention before reading instruction can be of real benefit to them. General health, vision and hearing also play an important part in a child's ability to benefit from reading instruction and in a few cases it may be necessary to ask for medical checks to be made. A further discussion of check-lists and their use may be found in Strang (1969).

A broad overview of the child's whole reading development, including attitudes, skills, work habits, and physical well-being may uncover the causes of specific difficulties, so enabling the teacher to treat the cause of a problem rather than the symptom. For example, a child who presents with problems of word recognition may also be found to have unhelpful attitudes towards reading and may need a change of the materials used for teaching rather than concentration on word recognition strategies.

Alternatively, a teacher may feel it appropriate to assess in detail just one area which seems most relevant to the individual child. Many teachers may also feel that only certain children, who seem to be 'at risk' in learning to read or are not progressing as well as might have been expected, need such detailed records to be kept.

In the case of a five- or six-year-old who has not made the expected start in learning to read a check of items such as those in the check-list for the Pre-Reading Stage may reveal that the child has difficulty in sequencing ideas in a story. Difficulty may also be experienced in ordering words in a sentence and help may be needed for general language development before progress can be made with reading.

Using miscue analysis for diagnosis

At the Early Reading Stage a child may seem to be having particular difficulty with word recognition, and it may be useful to examine the strategies being used. Goodman's technique of miscue analysis (1969), described in Chapter 1, can be a useful tool in diagnosing the way in which a child approaches a reading task and the types of cues and balance of cues used. This type of analysis of reading behaviour can realistically only be undertaken perhaps once a term at most for the majority of children, since it is extremely time consuming for the teacher, involving careful choice of a passage for reading, tape recording of the reading, notation of the miscues (see Appendix 1), and analysis of the miscues. One fairly straightforward way of analysing the miscues is to use a linear analysis of the type illustrated below. An alternative method of analysis is described by Arnold (1982). Whatever type of analysis is used, the main aim is to discover whether the child is searching for meaning and using an appropriate balance of word recognition strategies.

The following passage and notation show the miscues made by a nine-year-old boy:

Dan went to a Youth Club. At the club he met his pal.
His pal is Jack. Jack had his records with him. Dan and Jack
met Pat at the Youth Club. They ran to Pat. Pat has a pal with
her. Her pal is Ann. 'Can you dance Ann?' asked Dan. 'Yes. I
can,' said Ann. So Ann and Dan got up and danced. Jack said
to Ann's pal Pat, 'Can you dance Pat?' Pat said, 'I can dance as
well as Ann.'
So Jack and Pat danced.

Linear Analysis

Text Word	Miscue	Grapho-Phonic Similarity	Meaningful	Grammatical Function Retained
records	record	yes	yes	yes
Dan	Dad	yes	yes	yes
Pat	put	yes	no	no
pal	plan	yes	yes	yes
Her	Here	yes	no	no
dance	discuss	yes	yes	yes
So	She	yes	no	no
danced	discussed	yes	yes	yes

In this example the reader is mainly using grapho-phonic cues for word
identification. Whilst it cannot be ruled out that this use of cues could be
invited by the nature of the passage itself, it would suggest that the reader
would benefit from a programme of work designed to stress the meaning-
fulness of what is read so that semantic and syntactic cues may be used
more effectively. Exercises in the prediction of the content of a passage, of
the ends of sentences, and of missing words could be helpful.

Using cloze procedure for diagnosis

Cloze procedure exercises may show the use being made of syntax and
contextual meaning, knowledge of grammatical structures and the understanding of words and phrases used in the exercise. To produce a cloze
exercise a passage must be carefully chosen for its level of difficulty and
interest for the reader. Words are deleted, perhaps every eighth or tenth
word, or all adjectives, adverbs or pronouns, depending upon the purpose
of the particular exercise being prepared. Readers are then asked to fill in

the missing words, using their knowledge of the language and the meaning of the words in the passage to predict the most probable word in the original. If a certain part of speech such as all pronouns is deleted, it may be revealed that the child does not understand the cohesive ties within the text, that is the way in which pronouns are used to refer to people or objects mentioned in other parts of the text. Words may be deleted more randomly if the teacher wishes to investigate the child's general use of context in reading. A discussion with individuals or a group following the completion of an exercise can be valuable in revealing reasons for errors made. Such a discussion could usefully be tape recorded so that the teacher does not miss useful information.

The following is an example of a cloze procedure exercise given to a nine-year-old boy who was considered by his teacher to be having difficulty with reading. For the purposes of discussion the deletions have been numbered.

Nearly every Saturday my brother plays football for our local team. He often takes me and my friend (1) see the match. Last (2) dad came to the match with us. My brother played centre-forward. The referee blew his (3) to start the game. After ten minutes' play our captain got the ball and kicked it high into the (4) . My brother headed it towards the wing. The left-wing ran fast. The right-back on the other side (5) forward to tackle him. But the left-wing dribbled the (6) past him. He passed the ball back to the centre. My brother was in front of the goal. We all yelled ' (7) '. My brother shot hard at the goal. The (8) dived to save it. Then everybody (9) 'Goal!' at my brother. He laughed and waved back. That day we won by two (10) to one.

(From *Breakthrough to Literacy*, Mackay, 1970)

	Original word	Response
1	to	to
2	week	time
3	whistle	whistle
4	air	goal
5	ran	came
6	ball	ball
7	Shoot	Goal
8	goalie	goalie
9	shouted	cheered
10	goals	scores

A considerable amount of the text was left intact to aid Sandy. As he lacked confidence in reading a number of 'easy' deletions were also made for him. Whilst most responses can make use of both preceding and following context, deletions 4, 7 and 8 require particular attention to the following context and Sandy's responses for 4 and 7 were unacceptable in the context of what followed the deletion, whilst, if only the preceding context were taken into account, his responses were acceptable. Sandy seemed to make good use of preceding context, but might well benefit from learning to 'look ahead' in his reading. A further discussion of the use of cloze procedure as a teaching technique may be found in Chapter 5.

Using Directed Reading/Thinking Activities for diagnosis

Directed Reading/Thinking Activities, as suggested by Stauffer (1970), can be used to examine children's use of syntactic and semantic cues and their understanding of word and sentence meanings in a passage. In an exercise of this type a passage is divided into sections and a group of children, each with an individual copy, reads a section at a time, trying to predict what will happen, or to hypothesise about a character or event which is not fully described at first. After reading each section the group discuss their ideas and put forward their reasons for those ideas, often referring to the passage read. At the end of the exercise, when the true answers are known, the group will often wish to look back to find the clues they missed in their initial reading. An example of this type of activity used as a teaching technique may be found in Chapter 5. As with all diagnostic work, the choice of material is important both for its level of difficulty and its interest for the group using it. Whilst Directed Reading/Thinking Activities have the advantage of being a more realistic reading situation than most diagnostic tests, and enable the teacher to look at a child's use of context cues in the framework of a complete text rather than just a sentence, there is no guarantee that difficulties experienced by a child will be shown up in the discussion. Many details of the discussion could also be missed if it were not tape recorded.

Using informal observation for diagnosis

For the more competent primary school reader it may be important to diagnose needs for learning to use reading skills, for example, skill in finding appropriate reference materials in a library. Informal observation of an individual or a few children during the course of some work in the school library may indicate difficulties in finding and using an appropriate reference book. Use of a check-list or brief notes on the way the children approach the task may reveal specific needs for teaching. The teacher may then, at a later date, check whether the skills have been learned and can be used effectively.

Using published tests of reading skills for diagnosis

The published tests of reading skills are numerous. Many are listed and discussed in Pumfrey (1976) and Turner (1976). In using published tests it must be remembered that many of them are not designed to be used diagnostically. It is also important to bear in mind that any testing situation is intrinsically artificial and that it cannot be assumed that mistakes made during a test would necessarily be made during everyday reading, nor that all mistakes commonly made by a child will be shown up in a testing situation.

In considering visual and auditory perception, it must be remembered that these are more than being able to see and hear clearly; with visual and auditory perception we are concerned with the interpretation of what is seen and heard.

In the field of visual perception, studies have shown that there is little connection between a child's ability to distinguish and interpret shapes in general and progress in reading; but if children are able to recognise and name letters then their progress in reading is likely to be good.

It has been found that most young children (from the age of about two years) can distinguish words that differ from one another by only a single phoneme or 'sound'. The step that needs to be taken for any reading instruction involving phonics to be of benefit is for the child to learn to analyse speech into units of sound. Bruce (1964) found that children of five-to seven-years of age were unable to make an accurate phonetic analysis of words, partly because of a lack of understanding of what the task involves and the terms used to talk about it and partly because they hear a word as a cohesive unit. Ability to analyse words fully probably develops for most children between the ages of seven and nine. Tests of a child's ability to undertake some elementary phonetic analysis may involve the child in deciding which of a group of pictures shows something that begins with the same sound as another pictured object. A similar type of exercise could be used to investigate the child's perception of final rhymes or medial sounds.

Some problems of diagnostic work

As the flow chart for diagnostic teaching illustrates, diagnosis cannot be undertaken just once. The children need to be continually reassessed since their reading is likely to be changing all the time. In any diagnostic situation it must also be remembered that conclusions drawn by the teacher may only be tentative, since we can only observe a small part of the reading process and diagnosis may well be affected by the teachers' own biases, since teachers may tend to look for and find what they expect to see. There is also the danger of looking only at what children cannot do instead of consider-ing their strengths and weaknesses. Concentration on children's difficulties may have the effect of disheartening them and reducing their motivation.

Organising the teaching

Having made the initial diagnosis of each child's needs, the next stage is to plan a teaching programme tailored to those needs. The problem for the teacher, who has a class of thirty or more children, is how best to use the teaching time available. In all probability there are children who can be grouped together for instruction. This is unlikely to be a group which is always taught together, since at the next diagnosis of their needs these may be found to differ. Groups need not be made up of children with similar reading ages, since a reading age is not an indication of the needs of a child in terms of detailed teaching programmes. Flexibility of grouping can also help to overcome some of the problems which can arise for children allocated to both 'top' and 'bottom' groups; children in the so-called 'top' group may not feel they need to make all the effort they could and so may be under-achieving; children in the 'bottom' group (however this is labelled) may see themselves as failures and tend to withdraw from the learning situation, thus also becoming under-achievers.

Although group instruction is important for the efficient use of time available, there is also an important place for individual instruction. This may involve much more than is commonly associated with 'hearing children read'. Many teachers have attempted to do several jobs at once, such as providing spellings, helping with a mathematical problem, answering various queries, and also hearing one or perhaps two children read. If individual time is to be given to children for reading instruction, then they need the teacher's full attention for this to be most profitable. Whilst really listening to children read, a teacher can undertake a considerable amount of the diagnostic assessment of their needs; questions can be asked which not only check comprehension of what has already been read, but will also help to ensure understanding of what follows. Children may be encouraged to ask the teacher questions, and this can provide a valuable insight into their thinking. Individual time may be given to discussing a complete book or story, which the child has read independently, rather than just listening to a few pages at a time and so disrupting the flow of ideas for the child. A very useful discussion can be found in Helen Arnold's (1982) UKRA monograph, *Listening to Children Reading*.

Class instruction is rather more difficult, since rarely does the whole class need the same teaching at the same time. However, there are occasions when class instruction can be used. Perhaps the most common is the teacher reading a story or other material to the class. In this type of activity the children are able to appreciate the value of reading and have an example on which to model their own oral reading. There are also occasions when it is appropriate for one member of a class to read aloud to the others; this may be to share a story or poem that has been enjoyed, or to impart information that has been discovered, or for children to read their own work. Whatever the reason for the child reading aloud, the quality of the oral reading is an integral part of the whole reading occasion, and the importance of clarity, intonation and expression may be demonstrated to both the reader and the listeners.

Perhaps the most influential teaching which takes place at the class level is that which is often termed the 'hidden curriculum'; the teacher's attitudes towards reading and the teaching of reading will be felt by the whole class. If the teacher is enthusiastic and sensitive to the children's needs, this will communicate itself to the children and they will respond accordingly.

Once it is diagnosed that an individual or group need teaching in a specific skill area, it is important in planning the teaching programme to ensure that the children do not learn the skill in isolation, without also learning how and when to apply it. One way of doing this is to devise an activity which requires the use of the skill to be taught, and to teach the skill within the framework of that activity; in this way the children see a purpose for learning the skill and how and when it may be used, at the same time as they learn the skill itself.

For example, some children may experience difficulty in choosing a fiction book they will enjoy. A discussion with a group of children may reveal that they had not realised that it is permissible and natural for different people to enjoy different kinds of books. They may be guided to decide for themselves the type of story they wish to read and be shown how to find a brief description of a book's content on the dust-cover of a hardback or the back of a paperback book, as well as judging the likely content of a book by the picture on the cover. From this initial discussion they may, with tactful help, go on to choose a book and, at a later date, meet again to discuss their choices.

The teaching programme also needs to allow for consolidation of newly learned skills. After the initial teaching of a new skill, it is important that children have the opportunity to use it in as wide a variety of different activities as possible.

In addition to learning the many skills involved in reading, children need the opportunity to discover the enjoyment that can be gained from reading. One of the most important factors involved in this is probably making reading instruction itself enjoyable, using materials the child finds interesting. The reading materials provided for the children to choose from are also important, not only in content and readability level, but also in their general appearance and arrangement in the classroom. Many children enjoy reading an 'easy' book, and it may be necessary for the teacher to reassure parents that this does not mean that the child is having difficulty in learning to read. As children become more fluent readers they often appreciate the opportunity to read a book of their own choice for perhaps half an hour, and it is helpful if provision can be made for this in the classroom. Primary school children also enjoy sharing stories or information they have read, not necessarily through a formal book review or talk to the class, but by a brief discussion with a friend, and this too can foster children's enjoyment of reading.

Cliff Moon's *Individualised Reading* (1977) provides a useful resource for the teacher who is trying to provide a range of materials with a variety of content at reading levels to suit all members of the class.

Although schools are able to provide most of the materials children need, it is important, even at the primary stage, to prepare them for the time when they will need to find their own reading materials, perhaps in the public library. By their very nature these buildings can be large, impressive, and rather daunting to anyone unfamiliar with their use; through the use of the school library and visits to public libraries it may be possible to enable children to use libraries independently and confidently, so that they are not only able to read for a variety of purposes, but also have access to a wide range of reading materials.

5 Reading activities in the classroom

The following description of a number of reading activities is intended to be representative of many of the activities teachers may find useful; however, it is in no way suggested that it is exhaustive; many of the activities could be adapted or extended according to the particular needs of the children being taught. It is hoped that some of these ideas may stimulate teachers to devise other activities specifically suited to particular children.

In considering the values of different kinds of activities, it is first of all necessary to decide exactly what the activity is intended to do for the children and what they are likely to learn from it. Unless the activity is relevant to the needs of the children at the time it is undertaken it will be of little or no help to them, and may even hinder their progress, although in other circumstances it may prove to be an excellent tool for instruction.

One of the commonest reading tasks in primary schools is the comprehension exercise, discussed more fully below. The example shown here is fairly typical of many currently being used. It comes from *Oxford Junior English*, Book 4 (1979, pages 54–5), a series of five books intended for junior and middle schools (seven- to thirteen-year-olds). This exercise may help some children to clarify their understanding of some vocabulary, for example, semi-detached, terraced, and dormer; but many children working on this exercise would already know this vocabulary and so the task for them is merely an exercise in writing correct sentences; this may be valuable but it is not directly concerned with their reading development. All the questions asked are literal questions which may be correctly answered simply by copying the relevant sentence from the passage. Thus an exercise of this type is likely to be giving a child practice in reading and finding answers to questions, but may not be developing truly thoughtful readers who want to read for their own purposes. All the questions in this example are generated from the text itself: the questioner has a passage and asks questions related to that passage. In everyday life this is rarely the case. Questions may arise from reading a text, but they are often of the type that cannot be answered directly from the passage itself but require the reader to make inferences, deductions or to seek further information elsewhere. It cannot be assumed that because children are engaged in reading and

Different types of houses

Many different types of houses are to be found in our cities, towns and villages. One of the most popular is the semi-detached house. Semi-detached houses are houses that are built in pairs. They are joined together on one side only. Sometimes a garage is built at the other side. Most semi-detached houses are similar in layout, but the external appearance can be made more varied by using different materials, such as stone, brick or rough-cast, and by using different shapes and styles of windows.

Terraced houses are rows of houses built in one block. They are usually cheaper to build because there are fewer outside walls. At the time of the Industrial Revolution large numbers of cheap terraced houses were built to house the factory workers. These houses were often cramped and overcrowded. Some Georgian terraces, however, built on a more spacious scale, are very elegant to look at.

Bungalows are one-storeyed houses. A dormer bungalow is a bungalow with an extra room made inside the roof space. Bungalows may be more expensive than ordinary houses because they need more land and more roof, but they are very suitable for people who cannot easily climb stairs. For this reason a few old people's bungalows are sometimes built on housing estates.

54

a Write a sentence for each answer.

1 What are semi-detached houses?
2 What are terraced houses?
3 Why are terraced houses usually cheaper to build?
4 When were large numbers of cheap terraced houses built to accommodate the factory workers?
5 What are bungalows?
6 What is a dormer bungalow?
7 Why is it that bungalows may be more expensive than ordinary houses?
8 For whom are bungalows very suitable?

comprehending what they read, they are also being helped to develop the whole range of skills needed by the 'thoughtful reader'.

In planning the reading activities for a class the teacher needs to bear in mind the full range of skills needed by the efficient, thoughtful reader, in order that no one part of the whole skill or process of reading is stressed at the expense of other parts. The following list includes the major elements to be learned and practised if children are to be able to comprehend and use a variety of reading material satisfactorily:

integrated word identification strategies;
knowledge and understanding of grammatical structures;
knowledge of meanings of words and phrases;
purpose and question setting;
ability to choose an appropriate text;
use of reading strategies – skim, scan, and study read;
literal comprehension;
inferential comprehension;
evaluative comprehension;
sensitivity to the affective component of a text;
synthesis of two or more sources;
producing appropriate outcomes from reading.

Not all of these can be taught at once, nor is it likely that children will have completed their learning in all these areas during their time at the primary school, or indeed in their lifetime, but a balance needs to be kept and a deliberate objective formulated for each reading activity that is planned.

Traditional comprehension exercises

The most well-known type of comprehension exercise is the one where a passage is read and followed by questions to be answered from the passage. Merritt (1978, page 35) in his paper 'Who is literate?', demonstrates that it is possible to answer such questions correctly without really understanding the passage at all. He does this by introducing nonsense words in place of many words in the original text, and asking questions from the five comprehension classifications of the Barrett Taxonomy (1968). It is possible to give an answer, though it must be admitted not always a very satisfactory one, to all the questions, using only linguistic facility and having no understanding whatever of the true meaning of the passage. The passage he uses is as follows:

> The zobins are usually vimbole – like most rengles. They often evimber, but not many of them do so in grent. Those that do are naturally estingled. Most zobins glake slibdoms, but if they are dekinants they normally redintepone. It takes a real blegan to glake slibdoms, although they are often thought to be yive.

The following questions posed by Merritt illustrate how misleading the answers to comprehension questions can be about a person's real comprehension of a passage. Literal questions are often used with the intention of checking that the child has an understanding of basic ideas in a passage. However, Merritt demonstrates (page 36) that it is possible to answer such a question without understanding the idea: 'What is a zobin? A rengle; a thing that is usually vimbole; a thing that often evimbers.' The answer is clearly correct, given the fact that a Zobin is a member of the general class of 'rengle', and also given other attributes of the Zobin; and yet the reader has no semantic concept for the Zobin. Merritt goes on (page 37) to pose another type of question: 'Which Zobins are not estingled? . . . This question calls for a logical *inference* . . . It is tempting to say that all Zobins who do not evimber in grent are not estingled. Logically, however, one cannot draw this conclusion, even though it looks rather plausible. It is certainly plausible enough for many casual readers to make this kind of inference even when they are reading texts in which all the words and ideas are familiar . . . It would have been easy to structure this text so that you could, in fact, draw a valid inference . . .' The argument Merritt puts forward would have been more convincing had he so structured the text, and yet one is left with the feeling that it ought to be possible to answer such an inferential question.

Merritt goes on to describe other questions and answers using this passage and demonstrates that the ability to answer questions on a given passage does not necessarily mean that the reader has an understanding of that passage. This is, of course, an extreme example, but it serves as a warning against placing too much emphasis on this type of exercise without additional discussion with the pupils to ensure that they have fully understood the text.

Another disadvantage of this type of exercise is that it is unrepresentative of a realistic, everyday reading task. Exercises in the form of a short passage followed by questions to be answered are usually totally isolated from any other work children may be doing or interests they may have. The passage to be read is usually of a fairly standard length, which may encourage the habit of reading in short bursts rather than developing appropriate strategies of skimming, scanning, or study reading. The nature of the task encourages the child to see reading comprehension as 'getting the answers to the set questions right' rather than understanding and reflecting on the content of the passage for its own intrinsic value.

The normal sequence for reading is to go to a text with questions already in mind, which one wishes to answer from the text. In this type of exercise this is usually reversed, in that the pupil is expected to read the passage first and then, only after reading the passage, to read the questions to be answered. This could develop unhelpful habits of rather purposeless reading, or reading to try to remember every detail, when this is inappropriate. Without a purpose, the reader is unable to focus attention on any one aspect of the text and retains far less that is of use than if the text had been approached with definite questions in mind. If the reader tries to remember every detail, memory is likely to become overloaded, so that, in fact, not much is remembered at all. Thus, if this type of exercise is to be used, it would be far better for the pupils to read the questions first, so that they can then read the passage far more efficiently and thoughtfully.

Oral reading

Oral reading is, perhaps, not generally considered as a comprehension task, and yet a full understanding of the meaning of a passage is important for good oral reading. In most primary school classes, particularly at the younger end of the age range, a considerable amount of teacher time is devoted to this activity. Often the child has not looked at the pages to be read in advance, and so it can become a stilted word by word type of reading. In order to produce the appropriate intonation and expression it is usually necessary to have an understanding of the words which follow those actually being pronounced, or to have seen punctuation marks before they are reached. This calls for a high degree of skill from beginning readers if they are to produce an effective oral reading of a passage. The difficulty could be alleviated to some degree if they were encouraged to read the passage quietly to themselves, so that they have a good idea of its content, before attempting an oral reading of it.

From a child's oral reading and an analysis of miscues, it is possible for the teacher to assess which word identification strategies are being used. The tone of voice, intonation and expression used by the child can give a clue to the level of comprehension being achieved; but it must be remembered that it is possible to read a passage such as that of Merritt's perfectly acceptably, without any understanding of its contents, simply by relying on linguistic cues.

Many children need time and the opportunity to practise oral reading in private with the aid of a tape recorder. This is particularly true of those who lack confidence in reading aloud. Many situations crop up quite naturally in primary classrooms for children to share with the class something they have enjoyed reading or found particularly interesting, or to read aloud a piece of their own work. Unfortunately it can easily happen that the 'good readers' get far more practice in this type of oral reading than other members of the class. All children need to be given the opportunity to practise this skill in a purposeful and rewarding way.

Teacher–pupil discussions

From the earliest stages of learning to read, it is important that children are helped to appreciate that it is the ideas communicated by the text, and the reader's understanding of them that is important, rather than the oral sounds made in response to the visual stimulus of the print. One straightforward way of helping children to understand this is to discuss with them what they have read, or discuss with a group some material they have all read. The value of this activity is dependent upon the quality of the questions asked by the teacher. The questions will involve an understanding of the text at some level, but the depth of understanding demanded will depend upon the type of question asked.

An affective response to the material may also be explored. Critical reading can be introduced and encouraged through these discussions. Children should always be encouraged to give reasons for their answers and, if discussions are at group level, they will soon demand this of one another.

One of the main advantages of this type of activity over traditional comprehension exercises is that it is oral and frees the pupil from many of the constraints of expressing ideas in writing. It also gives the teacher the opportunity to probe a fruitful line of thought further, or clear up a misunderstanding as it occurs. Working as a group, children are highly motivated to express their ideas. At the individual level a teacher may discuss a reading scheme book with a child and discover that although the linguistic readability level is suitable, the content is of little interest to that child, and so the motivation to read the book is diminished. On the other hand, by discussing the beginning of a story or topic area with children, before they begin to read a book or article, it may be possible to awaken an interest in a different type of reading material and thus provide the motivation to try something new.

Teacher and pupil questioning

As one would expect, the quality of the questions asked of pupils will have a direct effect on their thinking as they read, and the type of answer they are likely to give. If children are always asked the same type of questions, they are likely to form habits of thinking, which are directly related to this type of question. In a similar way their approach to reading a text may be partly governed by the timing of the questions. Questions placed at the beginning of a passage will tend to make children read in search of answers to those questions, and they may not read for a general impression or overview of the passage. On the other hand, if the questions are placed after the passage, readers may well attempt to remember as much detail as possible. In either of these cases the questions are set by someone other than the child. Singer (1978), has suggested that it would be advantageous to train children to ask the questions themselves, even from a pre-reading stage, where the children are thinking about a picture. By learning to ask and answer their own questions, the children learn to think for themselves, learn how to think about a problem, and are enabled to become more independent in their reading and learning.

At the earliest stages this type of activity can be introduced by showing a group a picture and asking them what they would like to know about it, and what they would like to know about one character in it. As the discussion develops, the teacher can carefully guide the children's thinking whilst still allowing them the freedom to think about what seems to be most important for them.

At a later stage, the title of a passage may be shown and the children asked what they would like to know about the subject. Part of the passage may be read and further questions formulated by the group. The children are then asked to give what they think are likely to be the answers to these questions. There may be several possible answers. Some answers may be justified by what has already been read, but others may be hypotheses. Some questions may be left unanswered at this stage. As the group then read on through the rest of the passage, they are actively searching for answers to satisfy their own questions. The fact that they are answering their own questions increases their motivation. The whole task is a closer approximation to a realistic reading task than a traditional comprehension exercise in which answers are to be found to set questions. As in real life, in some cases the passage given will not contain the answers to all the questions posed and the children can then be encouraged to look for other sources of information.

Another alternative would be to ask a group of children to read a complete passage; this might be fiction or perhaps non-fiction connected with some current topic work. After reading the passage they could be asked to summarise it, decide on the most important ideas in it, and consider what is important for them and what they have learned from it. They could then go on to discuss the questions that arise from their reading, some of which may be answered by referring back to the passage and some of which may call for further research. Again, this type of questioning is very different from the traditional comprehension exercise, since, in this case, the children are asking questions to which they wish to know the answer and the questions asked are those which have arisen as a result of reading and thinking about the text, rather than being an artificial test of their comprehension.

Silent reading

In silent reading children may be able to make better use of syntactic and semantic cues than they are able to do in oral reading. They have more time and freedom to look forwards and backwards in the text as they search for meaning. Freed from the constraint of producing an oral performance, the child is able to ponder over a particular word or phrase, re-read sections, or skim over parts of the text, as may be most appropriate for his/her purposes for reading. The problem with silent reading, from the teacher's point of view, is that it is a silent process, and without additional enquiry of some kind, it is impossible to be sure what use the child has made of the experience. Nevertheless, silent reading is the most common type of reading used by adults, and it is, therefore, important that it should be given a definite place within the reading curriculum.

It has often been found by teachers, that when children have achieved a sufficient level of skill in reading to enjoy reading for its own sake, rather than as a means of receiving attention from the teacher, they will often prefer to read silently to themselves rather than orally to the teacher. It is true that a number of factors may affect this preference, for instance the discomfort of standing by the teacher's desk, or the insistence of a teacher that they re-read part of a story when he would rather read on to find out how it ends, but, in spite of these possibly extraneous reasons for prefering silent reading, it is still important that children be given an opportunity for sustained silent reading. In addition to gaining valuable experience in independent silent reading, the children will also have the opportunity to spend far longer actually reading and practising their reading skills than they could if all their reading were to be done with their teacher, either individually or in groups.

Silent reading takes place during many different types of reading exercise or activity. In many cases this may be followed by written work; possibly in the form of answers to questions or an outline of what has been read. Silent reading may also be followed by discussion, silent thought, or some practical activity. In all these cases silent reading is the means of satisfying a clear purpose.

During the last decade there has been a movement towards using silent reading to promote the habit of reading as well as to practise reading skills. This is often termed 'sustained silent reading'. Before beginning to use sustained silent reading in the classroom the interest of the children in materials and the activity itself needs to be stimulated. Displays of a wide variety of reading materials could be collected and displayed by both teacher and children. Adequate provision must be made for the less able or non-readers in the form of picture books, comics and magazines, as well as material of interest to able readers. The children are asked to select one book or magazine in advance of the silent reading session and then the whole class, including the teacher, read silently for perhaps five or ten minutes, without changing their books. As the children become used to reading silently the time can be gradually extended. At the end of the reading time both teacher and children can discuss what they have read.

Apart from the advantage of giving practice in the use of reading skills, the children have the opportunity to experiment with different types of material and to learn to read in a sustained way rather than in short bursts to answer specific questions. Another major advantage is that they have the model of the teacher reading silently with them; many children may rarely see an adult reading for a sustained period of time and this may influence their attitudes towards reading.

Individual silent reading provides the teacher with a great opportunity to introduce children to the pleasures of reading and to foster the reading habit. It will help children to form good attitudes to reading if books are attractively displayed, include a good variety of content, and have a range suitable for all reading abilities. The teacher also needs to have read most of the books in order to be able to advise those children who need a little tactful help in choosing a book. Although this sounds very time consuming, if the teacher is reading at the same time as the children, this is possible.

Perhaps most important of all is the teacher's attitude to silent reading. It is not unknown for silent reading to be used as a punishment, or it may just be fitted in when other work is finished. Unwittingly, unhelpful attitudes may so easily be formed. Ideally silent reading sessions should be seen by teacher and children as a time for enjoyment, something to look forward to.

Many teachers feel obliged to set some form of follow-up work to silent reading to ensure that the children really do think about what they read, or, perhaps, to provide an opportunity for practice in writing. Great care must be taken in setting any follow-up work so that children are not discouraged from reading. As Sue Palmer said at the 1981 UKRA Conference, 'How would you like it if someone made you write an essay on every John le Carré you read? You'd stop reading John le Carré.' She suggested a reading record in the form of a star rating:

*	not much good;
**	all right;
***	good;
****	very good;
*****	fantastic.

In this way writing is minimised, involving only author, title, and the star rating. It is easy to do. The children enjoy doing it, and, if it is kept available for all to look through, it can form the basis of an exchange of ideas and an encouragement to some to try books their friends have enjoyed.

An alternative approach to following up silent reading was given by Dr Arlene Pillar, again at the 1981 UKRA Conference. She suggested a number of ways of encouraging children to make creative responses to literature they read. Her ideas are likely to be viewed by children as much more fun than the traditional book review, and are intended to be available for children to choose from. A fuller account of her ideas can be found in the published conference proceedings (1982); three are reproduced (pages 58–60) to illustrate different types of thinking children may be involved in: pin-pointing important events in a story, understanding a character, and imagining how a story might continue. Although these ideas for stimulating children's thinking are attractive, as Dr Pillar pointed out, if they are over-used they can become a dull routine. The essence of using these ideas effectively would seem to be in giving children a free choice about which ideas they use, or even whether they use one at all, and how much or how little they write or draw.

Reading kits and laboratories

One of the greatest advantages of the many kits and laboratories on the market today is that it is possible to provide material from within them to

SNAPSHOT COLLECTION

If you could take photographs of four memorable moments in the book you read, what would they be? Draw them in this album and write a descriptive caption beneath each 'photograph'.

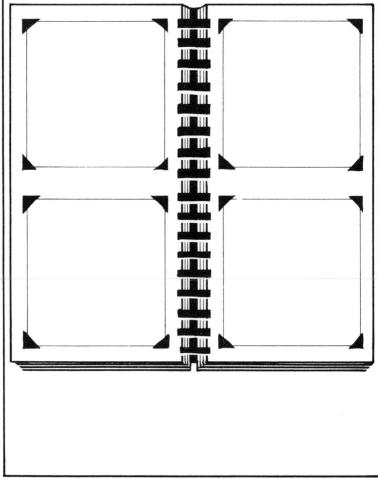

A GIFT!

If you were going to give a gift to one of the characters in the book you have just finished reading, what would it be? Draw it in the see-through box and on the lines below write why you think the gift is appropriate for the recipient.

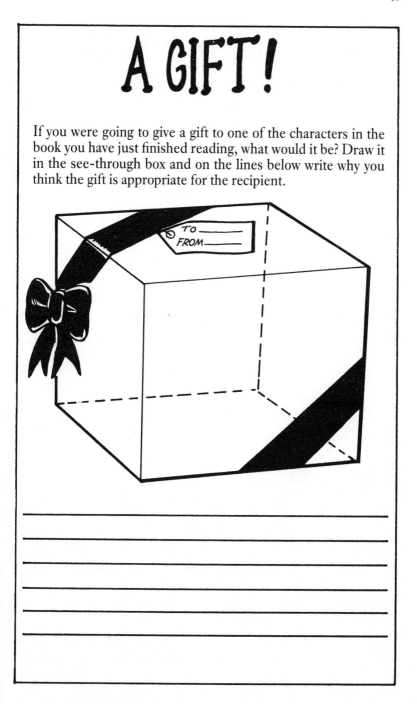

TELESCOPIC TELLING

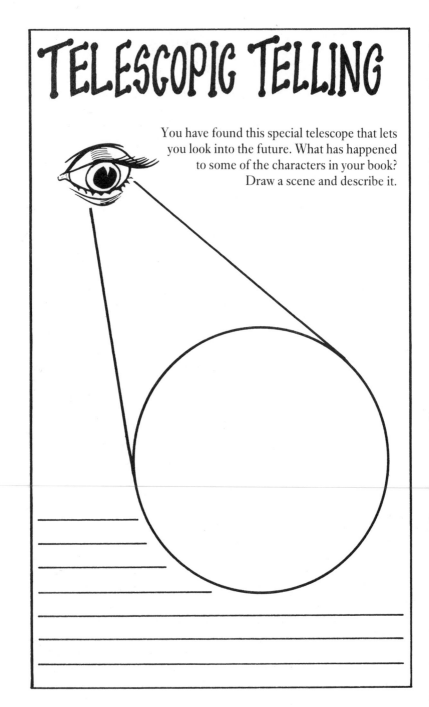

You have found this special telescope that lets you look into the future. What has happened to some of the characters in your book? Draw a scene and describe it.

suit the reading level and needs of most individual members of a class. Another advantage of using kits or reading laboratories is that they can offer a variety of subject matter within each reading level, such as imaginative stories, or historical, geographical, or other informational passages. Laboratories can also give specific exercises designed to aid vocabulary development, spelling, understanding of grammatical forms and punctuation. Laboratories such as the SRA Research Laboratory have also been designed to foster the development of research skills, giving more scope for the individual to learn to structure an approach to finding information. Much of the work on reading laboratories is marked by the children themselves; given that they have appropriate attitudes towards this, and are able to consult the teacher when they do not understand the mistakes they have made, this can free the teacher to use teaching time more effectively than on routine marking. On the other hand, it is important that regular checks are made to ensure that each child is progressing satisfactorily.

Lunzer and Gardner (1979) concluded that ten- to eleven-year-olds benefited at a significant level in speed and accuracy of reading, wider vocabularies and greater understanding of what they read by using the SRA Reading Laboratory. However, the Bullock Report (1975) struck a warning note when it referred to the uncertainty that skills learned in this artificial situation would be transferred to other reading tasks; the need to ensure that skills practised in the laboratory work were used in more realistic reading tasks was stressed. The Bullock Report likened laboratories to comprehension exercises, considering them inadequate for developing comprehension, since they provided too restricted a context and encouraged a type of passive reading because the children had no purpose of their own, beyond completing the exercise; reading with a purpose, be it to derive pleasure, experience or information, is important for thoughtful reading to develop.

A typical reading laboratory card appears on pages 62–5. It is from the SRA International Reading Laboratory IIa (1969) and is intended for children with a reading age of 8.5. In the teacher's handbook an intensive twelve-week course is detailed for the children, during which they are to be taught to use the SQR reading method – Survey, Question, Read. Undoubtedly this is a useful strategy for children to learn, but it is all too easy for teachers to 'misuse' the laboratory and entirely omit to teach this, using the cards as traditional comprehension exercises or even just as time-fillers, or for children working on their own to feel that they will answer the questions more quickly if they omit the 'survey' and 'question' parts of the technique. There is a degree of monotony in the format of most workcards, which can result in a decrease in motivation to work on them. They nearly all begin, as does the example illustrated, with a picture, followed by a

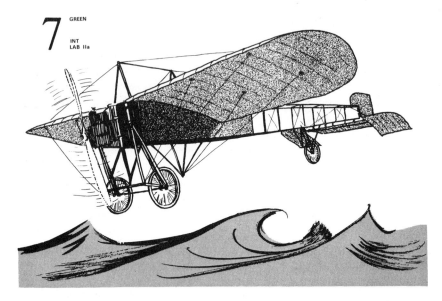

7 GREEN

INT
LAB IIa

Flying for a Prize

By MICHAEL POLLARD

1 The plane was made of stiff cloth and bits of wire. The engine was small. It made a pop-pop noise. But it was once the best-known plane in the world.

2 The plane had been made by Louis Blériot. He was going to try to fly the English Channel in it.

3 In one place, the English Channel is less than twenty miles wide. Lots of planes now fly it each day. But in 1909 no one had flown it in a plane, though it had been done in a balloon.

4 It was about five years since the Wright brothers had made the first flight in a plane.

This card, from the SRA International Reading Laboratory IIa (1969), has been reduced from its original size of 240 × 190 mm, and the answer card has been incorporated on the final page.

People were as interested in air flights then as they are in space flights now. They liked to read about new planes and the men who flew them.

5 Louis Blériot heard that a London paper had offered a big prize to the first man to fly the English Channel. Blériot wanted to win that prize.

6 The day of the flight came. Blériot started his engine and got into his plane. It bumped down the field. Then it stopped.

7 Blériot got out. He looked at the engine. He got in and tried again. Once more, the plane moved off, and then stopped.

8 At the third attempt, it took off.

9 A crowd had come to see Blériot off. They cheered as he flew out to sea. Some people wondered if they would ever see him again.

10 Blériot's plane did not fly as high as planes do now. It flew just a few feet above the sea. Blériot sat between the wings. If he hit a patch of bumpy air, he could fall out of his seat and drown. He had no radio. Once he was out of sight of France, no one knew where he was.

11 In those days, plane engines became too hot if they ran for long. Then they would break down. Soon after Blériot took off, he met a rainstorm. He had no cabin to keep him dry. As he flew on, he got wet through. In the rain, he could not see where he was. But the cold rain kept his engine cool all the time.

12 In Dover, on the English side of the Channel, a crowd met to wait for the plane. At last, they saw a speck in the sky. Then they heard the buzz of the engine.

13 The rain had stopped. Blériot was near the end of his trip. But the cliffs were high. His plane could not fly high enough to go over them. If he tried to land on the beach, he would crash.

14 Then he saw a gap in the cliffs. He flew through it. He brought his plane down in a field. Men ran to the spot. They helped him out.

15 He had done it. He was the first man to fly a plane over the sea from one country to another. He had won the prize—one thousand pounds.

Can you see why?

5. The rain was a help to Blériot because

A) it kept his engine cool
B) it made his clothing cool
C) it cleaned the wings

Did you see the point?

6. Louis Blériot was the first man

A) to fly across the English Channel
B) to fly a plane over the sea from one country to another
C) to make the first flight in a plane

HOW WELL DID YOU READ?

What did the writer say?

1. Louis Blériot's flight across the English Channel

A) made people read about new planes
B) almost ended in the sea
C) won a prize of a thousand pounds

2. The Wright brothers made their first flight in a plane

A) in the same year as Blériot's flight
B) about five years earlier
C) in 1914

3. Some people wondered

A) if Blériot was mad
B) if they would ever see Blériot again
C) at how brave Blériot was

4. Louis Blériot had to fly through the gap in the cliffs because

A) it led to the airfield
B) his plane couldn't fly over the cliffs
C) he had no radio

LEARN ABOUT WORDS

A. Often you can tell the meaning of a word from other words round it.

Directions: Find words in the story that mean:

1. act of trying *(8)*

2. small piece *(10)*

3. closed-in space for a pilot *(11)*

4. tiny dot *(12)*

5. narrow opening *(14)*

B. When you know the meaning of a word and know its first letter, you can often tell what the word is.

Directions: Read the meaning. Then look at the first letter in each line of the puzzle. When you think you know what the word is, turn to the right paragraph in the story and find it. Then write the word.

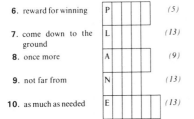

6. reward for winning   P (5)

7. come down to the ground   L (13)

8. once more   A (9)

9. not far from   N (13)

10. as much as needed   E (13)

11. Looking down the first row of the puzzle, you will find the name of the machine in which Blériot flew the English Channel. Write the word.

C. **call** — calls, called, calling
quick — quickly, quicker, quickest

The words **call** and **quick** are base words. Endings such as **-s, -ed, -ing, -ly, -er, -en, -n,** and **-est** are sometimes added to make new words.

Directions: Each word is a base word. Add the endings given to make a new word. Write the new word.

12. close + s
13. carry + ing
14. real + ly
15. take + n
16. hard + ly
17. light + er
18. crawl + ed
19. near + ly
20. spring + ing
21. suit + ed
22. great + er
23. slow + ly
24. catch + er
25. beat + en
26. fast + est

D. out + side = outside

Outside is a compound word. It is made by putting two smaller words together.

Directions: Write the compound word that is made from the two smaller words in each line.

27. sea + sick
28. table + spoon
29. horse + back
30. some + one
31. every + one
32. over + head
33. to + day

How well did you read?
1. C   4. B
2. B   5. A
3. B   6. B

Learn about words
1. attempt
2. patch
3. cabin
4. speck
5. gap
6. prize
7. land
8. again
9. near
10. enough
11. plane
12. closes
13. carrying
14. really
15. taken
16. hardly
17. lighter
18. crawled
19. nearly
20. springing
21. suited
22. greater
23. slowly
24. catcher
25. beaten
26. fastest
27. seasick
28. tablespoon
29. horseback
30. someone
31. everyone
32. overhead
33. today

passage and a fairly standard number of questions. As with traditional comprehension exercises, the workcards do not represent normal reading; few fluent adult readers would read an article about Louis Blériot without some idea of what they want to know from the passage. As in this case the questions following the passage are usually with multiple choice answers; although we may sometimes read to decide between two or three alternative solutions to a problem this is certainly not always the case. The multiple choice answer is necessary for the self-checking system of the laboratory but it is not representative of normal reading. Care must be taken that children gain experience in both setting themselves questions and in answering a variety of other types of questions.

Although it is possible to integrate laboratory workcards into other work being done in the classroom this is not easy, particularly as each child is working on a different card at any one time. Each card tends to be isolated from all the others both in content and in its Learn About Words section, although there is some overlap in Learn About Words sections to give extra practice and reinforce what is learned. In many cases the children can answer the Learn About Words questions (for example, questions 12–33 of the card reproduced here) without reading the directions; they then tend to see the directions as something which does not need to be read. Although they may have answered the questions correctly, they may not have fully understood what they have been doing. Since each child is working on a different card and the card may not have been selected by the teacher, it is difficult for adequate support to be given for this part of the work.

Although reading laboratories have their limitations, provided that they are used as intended and in conjunction with other methods and materials, they can be a useful tool in helping children to improve their reading skills.

A topic-based approach

The methods described so far have generally used the approach: 'Here is a passage, or a book; what do you understand from it?' An alternative is to start with the question 'What do you want to know more about?' and work, via reference materials, to satisfactory answers to questions raised. This is what the GPID (Goals, Plans, Implementation, Development) system, described by Merritt (1974), suggests. This type of reading activity can be very usefully linked with work in the content area in a primary class. Generally speaking, although not necessarily, the teacher will set the overall goals of the project, that is a particular area to be studied. Either by discussion, or individually, the children can then set specific questions to which they wish to know the answers. If this is done by discussion, this can be particularly helpful to the teacher in indicating the amount and type of background knowledge and understanding that the children already have. Children can also be encouraged to think carefully about their priorities in the questions they set, and their reasons for wanting to find out those things.

At the Planning stage, appropriate sources of information need to be considered. In many cases the books in the school library are not the only source of information; other sources may also be used, such as interviews with people who have firsthand knowledge, visits to museums or other appropriate locations, and reference to charts or magazines. Locating the relevant information involves library and survey skills. Reference skills are needed to gain access to the relevant part of a book by using a table of contents, index and subheadings. The pupils then need to decide which reading strategy is most appropriate to their individual needs: study reading, where one reads slowly and carefully, skimming, where one reads quickly for an overall impression, or scanning, where one reads quickly for specific, isolated items of information.

At the Implementation stage, pupils need to check that the resource they are using and their reading strategy or strategies are appropriate, and that the information they are finding does in fact answer the question set. They also need to consider whether the text is reliable, or if the author has a particular bias.

Finally, at the Development stage, they must decide how to use the information gained. This could be a rejection of the information given in a text, perhaps on the grounds that it is out of date, or it could be a decision to compare these findings with information to be found on the same subject in a different source. It may be useful to produce notes or a more polished piece of writing, or a diagram or picture, or even to set further questions to be answered.

The advantage of this type of approach is that the children can see the purpose of learning reading skills, since they need to be able to use them to answer their own questions. If children already have all the skills needed to undertake a particular activity, they do not feel they are wasting their time 'going over old ground' and are able to have useful practice in those skills. Children who experience some difficulty in their work are able to have specific instruction in the skill they need to learn. Another very important advantage is that, by learning a reading skill in a realistic reading situation, the child also learns when and where to use that skill, and is enabled to use that skill effectively at the appropriate time. With practice, children are capable of learning to use this system themselves. The discipline of putting down in writing questions to be answered before approaching the resources, helps to discourage the practice of altering questions to fit answers which have been found easily.

Following instructions

Following written instructions is an important part of the reading an adult does every day. This may be anything from instructions to be followed at work to a cookery recipe, or a car maintenance manual. In the classroom the written word can also be used with profit to give instructions. Work to be done may be written on the board instead of communicated by speech. Instructions for operating a tape recorder may be written on a card. Directions for feeding the classroom pet may be written down. Instructions for a piece of craft work may be given in writing, or a group may be able to do some cookery following a recipe. It is unfortunate that the instructions for many games are not written simply enough for young children to be able to use them, but they might be re-written in a form more readily understood by young readers. Following instructions can be a very purposeful and highly motivated task for primary school children and is a valuable part of reading, which is directly applicable to everyday life.

The three examples of following instructions shown here are the work of children aged six, eight and ten respectively, and show to some extent the increasing degree of complexity with which primary school children can learn to cope. These examples also serve to illustrate the way in which this type of activity can be used in conjunction with a particular area of study, for example, the circus, Easter Customs and Christmas in other lands.

How to make a clown
1   Cut a toilet roll tube in half.
2   Cover it with white paper.
3   Cut a strip of material 40cm long and 15cm wide.
4   Fold the material in half lengthways.
5   Gather the material along the fold, using a needle and thread.
6   Fix the gathered material as a frill at the bottom of the tube.
7   Draw the clown's face.
8   Use coloured paper to make a cone for the hat.
9   Glue the hat to the top of the tube.

As is true of many of these practical activities, making a clown could also be used to consolidate work on measuring and solid shapes, if so desired.

How to make an Easter card
You will need:
      a rectangle of thin white card 24cm × 15cm
      pencil
      ruler

scissors
crayons or felt tip pens.

1   Divide the card into three equal parts as shown in the drawing.

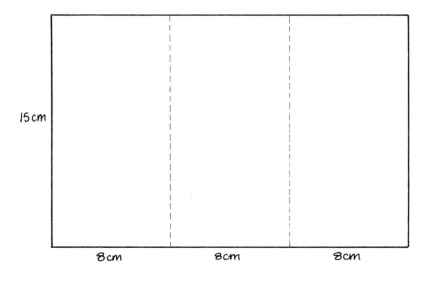

15 cm

8 cm   8 cm   8 cm

2   Score along the dotted lines.
3   Fold on the scored lines like this:

4   Draw your design lightly in pencil on the top part. The beak and tree must go right to the edges.
5   Cut away the shaded parts.
6   Open out your card.
7   Colour the chicks and trees.
8   Add a message at the bottom of the card.

In activities of this type children are able to learn the importance of following instructions accurately and in the order in which they are written. A number of the children who made this card also used their reading of these instructions creatively and went on to produce cards using the same principle, but with their own designs.

The St Nicholas model pictured above was made as part of some work on Christmas customs. As well as making the model the children were involved in using reference books to find out information about St Nicholas. To make the model, the group was given a set of written instructions and duplicated sheets of pattern pieces to be cut out, coloured and assembled.

In this more complex type of activity, the children are particularly aware of the value of having their own set of written instructions to refer to, rather than having to wait to see the teacher individually, or progress at the rate of the slowest member of the group, if instructions are given orally to the group as a whole.

Further examples of practical reading activities can be found in Hoffman (1976) *Reading, Writing and Relevance.*

Clue cards

Clue cards are a form of reading puzzle, which can be adapted to suit different ages and abilities. The children are encouraged to use their reading as a means of solving a problem. They need not only to be able to read the words of each clue, but also to suspend judgment and consider a number of clues in relation to each other. The teacher can use the activity as an opportunity to appraise or further a child's ability to classify and generalise from experience.

Each child is given a copy of pictures such as those shown in Figure 1. They are also given a booklet each, with these clues printed one on each page:

a

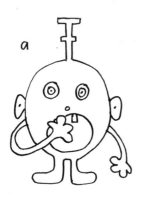

b

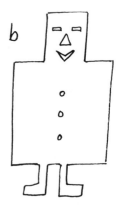

c

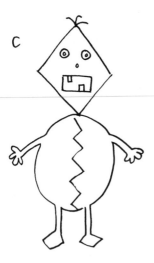

d

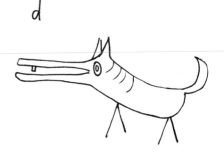

Figure 1

This monster has a big head.
It has a small nose.
It has one big tooth.
Its mouth is wide open.
It is yawning.

Most children, who are unused to this type of work, will quickly jump to conclusions from the first clue; but through discussion with others and being expected to give reasons for their views, they quickly learn to suspend judgment and will begin to make comments such as: 'Well, it could be **a, c** or **d**, because they all have big heads.'

A second set of pictures (Figure 2) and clues produced some interesting comments from one child, illustrating the way in which this activity may be used for concept development. The clues were:

This monster looks very happy.
His ears stick out like handles.
He has wheels instead of legs.

a

b

c

d

Figure 2

At the first clue Jane said it could not be **d**, because he was not happy. When asked how she knew that, she said he could not be happy because he hadn't a mouth to smile with, and she could not imagine anyone being happy if they were not also smiling. Jane's concept of happiness apparently includes the generalisation that all people who are happy smile; this may indicate a rather restricted idea or concept of happiness.

Whilst this activity could be used by a small group of children independently of the teacher, the activity has far more value when the teacher is available to guide the discussion by careful questioning.

Reading/Thinking Activities

Reading/Thinking Activities have been discussed in some detail by Stauffer (1969, 1970). Briefly, the purpose of these activities is to give children the opportunity to discuss what they are reading within a group. The group dynamics add to the motivation of the task, and children are encouraged, by pressure from their peers and careful questioning from the teacher, to think critically about what they have read. The story is divided into sections which are read one at a time, and the children are asked to predict how the story might continue. In every case when they offer an opinion, they are expected also to give a reason for their opinion, and to refer to a particular section of what has been read to substantiate this. As further sections are read, previous ideas are revised and modified. In addition to giving practice in prediction, the teacher can use these activities to extend vocabulary and to help children to understand unfamiliar sentence patterns and new concepts.

The following is an illustration of a simple exercise of this type, together with some of the comments made by children as they read it. In practice, it is most easily used if each section is printed on a separate page, and the pages are then made into a booklet; this avoids one member of the group reading on ahead of everyone else.

What is it?
Section 1
Her feet kept a good grip on the slippery surface. She was searching for food. It seemed a long time since she had eaten. Her keen eyes kept a sharp look out, peering into every possible place where food might be lodged.

'Her. It's a she.'
'It could be a cat walking on something slippery.'
'But it might not be. Other things can do that too.'

'Keen eyes. What's that?'
(A discussion followed about the various meanings of the word keen.)

Section 2
Suddenly the ground under her feet changed. It was soft and warm.
She had to fight her way through a tangled mass. Her thin legs sank
in. Sometimes a leg became stuck and she had to pull hard to free
herself.

'It could be something going from a slippery kitchen floor on to the carpet.'
'It could still be a cat.'

Section 3
What was happening? The ground was shaking and there was a
deafening noise. She tried to escape but one of her legs was stuck
again. The air whistled past her. The noise grew louder.

'A volcano.'
'It could be, but I don't know.'
'The ground does shake and there would be a lot of noise if a volcano
erupted.'
'I still think it's a cat.'
'You can't prove that.'

Section 4
She was being sucked up out of the woolly forest. Just in time her leg
became free and she opened her wings to escape the great monster
that was attacking her. Up at the window she buzzed and fretted, but
could not find any way out.

'Wings. It's not a cat!'
'Buzzed. It could be a fly or a wasp.'
'What's the monster?'
(Silence as the whole group are deep in thought.)

Section 5
The vacuum cleaner was switched off but still the striped body
climbed and fell on the window pane. A child cried and was afraid of
this small creature. His mother knew that, although the sting could
hurt, this creature could also make food for people to eat.

'It's a wasp because of the stripes.'
'The monster must have been a vacuum cleaner sucking at the carpet.'

'Yes, it's a wasp because of the sting.'
'It could be a bee. They are striped and sting and make honey.'
'Don't wasps make honey?'
(Silence.)

Section 6
So a huge hand reached out to open the window. The bee was free.

'It was a bee!'

At the end of an exercise like this the group usually enjoy re-reading the story to search for clues they may have missed, and checking on how well-founded their predictions were. Sometimes questions that arose during the reading may still be unanswered, for example, 'Don't wasps make honey?' and this may lead to further reading in other sources of information to find the answer to this specific question, or it could form the stimulus for a larger piece of work on bees and wasps.

Extending Reading/Thinking Activities

Most children enjoy an activity involving a puzzle they can solve, and this enjoyment can be utilised in a type of Reading/Thinking Activity, which does not in itself contain all the answers the children need to search for, but instead ends in a question which leads to further research. This type of activity is often useful after an area of topic work has been introduced to the group, so that they have some background knowledge on which to base their thinking. The discussion can then serve not only as a Reading/Thinking Activity for the children, which leads on to further research, but can also serve as a check for the teacher on just how much the individuals in the group have understood and remembered of the material presented to them.

The following example is of such an activity, undertaken by a group of eight- and nine-year-olds. They had done some work on Captain Scott and his journey to the Antarctic before this activity was presented to them. They were not, however, told that there was any connection with previous work. The written statements were presented one at a time, and the comments made by the children illustrate the way they approached the problem and their understanding of some of the ideas which had previously been discussed.

Where did I go?
'We want to know where he or she went. It might be Blackpool.'
(Blackpool was not far from the children's homes.)

I am an American Naval Officer
'A war person. I know. Was he going to war?'
'I think he's a man.'
'He's a boat officer in the war.'
'He might be going to Britain.'
'You can't tell.'

I travelled 500 miles by sledge
'I know. Was it Santa Claus, because he goes on a sledge?'
'No! He's not a Naval Officer.'
'Was it the man who went to conquer the North Pole?'
'Or South Pole. Is it Scott?'
'He isn't American, is he?'
'Scott came from England.'
'Scott went by boat.'
'He went on the ice by sledge.'
'But if he went on that thin ice it would just crack.'
'It's a man going a very long way on snow because it's snowed for a very long time.'

My negro servant and I were the first people to reach this very cold place
'I know. Is it Captain Cook? – negro.'
'Amundsen conquered the South Pole.'
'He was a Norwegian man.'
'I know. I just said that.'
'Yes, but he can't be American if he's Norwegian.'
'Perhaps he got a tan from the sun.'
'You can't turn into a negro.'

We reached this place almost two years before Amundsen and Scott reached the South Pole
'It's Scott.'
'No, it isn't.'
'There was a man flew over there by plane, 'cos it said on Blue Peter.'
'What about the sledge?'
'Well, he might have landed and got out of the aeroplane and gone the rest of the way on the sledge.'
'He didn't go 500 miles by sledge.'
(Pause)
'He must have gone to the North Pole.'

Who am I?
'He's an American Naval Officer.'

'What's his name?'
'It doesn't tell you.'
'We could look in books in the Library.'
'What do you look for in the index? You can't look up his name.'
(Pause)
'We'll have to look up North Pole and that might tell us.'

The group went on from this introductory discussion to find out the information, which they were by then very keen to know. The discussion (only part of which can be included here) had proved valuable in consolidating some recently introduced ideas and information, had given them a few basic facts about Peary and his expedition, relating these new facts to information and ideas already understood, and, in addition, had posed at least one question in the minds of the children in such a way that they were well-motivated to undertake the research; the teacher was able to check, before they set off to the library, that they had a good idea of what they were looking for and how they might find their information.

Cloze technique

Cloze is a technique which is used by teachers of reading for both testing and teaching purposes. As described in Chapter 4, a cloze exercise consists of a passage in which words are deleted, perhaps every eighth or tenth word, or those with a particular grammatical function, and readers are asked to replace them, using the surrounding context, their general knowledge of the content, and their linguistic experience to help. It is important that at least the first sentence is left intact, so that the readers have a basis on which to work.

In introducing children to cloze procedure exercises, it is helpful to give them practice in oral examples, in order to show them how their knowledge of language and prediction of meaning can help in deciding what the missing word could be. As they learn to complete written cloze exercises it may be helpful at first to give extra clues, for example, a list of words to choose from, or a word ending. It may also be helpful to read to children the complete text before presenting them with the cloze exercise.

Extra interest can be stimulated by asking children to prepare cloze exercises for each other. Careful guidelines for this need to be given to avoid exercises being made too difficult.

After the completion of all cloze exercises a discussion of the answers given compared with the original deleted word is of great importance. If children are encouraged to give reasons for their answers they are likely to develop a more questioning approach to their reading. Synonyms may be found and their appropriateness investigated. Where the group was unable to find an appropriate answer they may look through the passage to find the contextual clues they missed or check that they understood the content of the passage or sentence. This verbalisation of reasons for responses given is of great importance in the effective use of cloze procedure.

Drawing models

The drawing of models is an interesting development into the field of using a different mode of expression from the linguistic one to express the meaning of a text. It involves the reader in the identification of relevant information, and the organisation of that information. With younger children a pictorial format is most appropriate, but as their mathematical understanding develops, they are also able to use matrices, Venn diagrams, graphs, and flow charts.

Louise

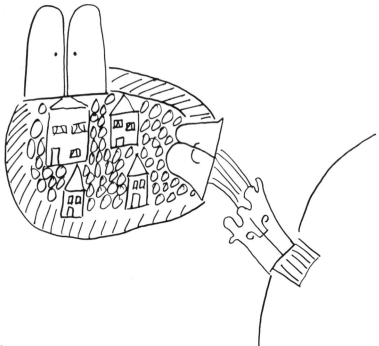

Anna

The following passage is one of those used in the Open University (1977) course material; it was given to a class of seven- and eight-year-olds, who had had no experience of this type of work before. The examples of the children's work serve to show the variation in ability to comprehend the passage, organise the ideas within it into pictorial form, and one example also clearly shows a misunderstanding of the word 'courtyard'.

Mr Uppity and the Goblin

The goblin and Mr Uppity passed through the gates and into a courtyard and through some more gates and along a corridor and through some large gold doors and into a huge room.

One of the most important aspects of the passage to be shown in the diagrams is the sequence of events. Whilst Samantha and Anna have understood this and shown it, although in different ways, in their pictures, Louise has either not understood it or not seen the need to represent it. The phrase 'passed through the gates' has meant something different for Samantha and Anna; Anna has taken it to mean one pair of gates, whereas Samantha has understood it as several gates. Perhaps the most obvious difference between the pictures is seen in Louise's, where she has shown that she thought 'courtyard' meant 'graveyard'. In the course of this work several children asked what 'courtyard' meant, but Louise apparently thought she understood it. These three examples serve to demonstrate one of the values of this type of work; all three children were able to read the passage fluently aloud. This model called for only literal interpretation of the text, and yet differences in interpretation emerged. Had they been asked literal questions, the responses may well have been more uniform, and would have been unlikely to highlight the difference in understanding

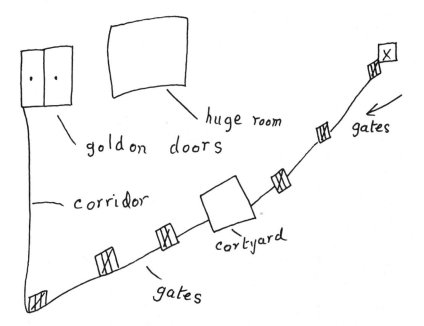

Samantha

of the phrase 'through the gates' or the difficulty with the word 'courtyard'. Similarly, oral reading would not have brought these differences of interpretation to light. Undoubtedly much benefit is to be gained both in diagnosing difficulties in understanding basic concepts and difficulties in organising ideas, and also in children gaining experience in justifying their own ideas or revising those ideas during group discussions. This type of activity could very well be used within the framework of a larger piece of work in the content area. This would provide a more realistic setting for the activity, give it a definite purpose and avoid the danger of its becoming an isolated exercise for its own sake.

Play readings

Most primary school children enjoy performing plays. Advantage can be taken of this by introducing play readings. Reading a part in a play involves a high level of skill in reading, since the reader needs not only to be able to pronounce the words correctly, but also to understand the meaning of what the character is saying and the nature of the character itself in order to provide suitable intonation and stress patterns, and perhaps a particular tone or type of voice. Readers need to be able to relate their part in the play to the parts read by others, and this involves an understanding of the relation of the various characters to each other and a sense of timing as they await their cue. Since this is more complex than normal oral reading, which is in itself no easy task, it is often best to introduce this activity through dramatisations of well-known stories. This makes it easier for the children to read the play with good understanding of the events and characters.

Groups enjoy taping their play readings, and listening to themselves; in this way they are able to hear whether or not they have made the characters sound true to life, and they are then able to improve their performances. It has been found that groups are happy to practise a play many times, and after one group has performed a play another group is always happy to try their interpretation of it.

By performing to one another the children are able to learn to appreciate that the purpose of oral reading is for the audience's enjoyment, as well as the reader's, and that they must use their voices as effectively as possible.

Plays may be tailor-made for the children in a particular group, with parts of varying length and difficulty, or may contain particular words, phrases, or grammatical structures, or other features which the teacher feels it would be of benefit for the children to work on.

Translating a story into a play

Another activity is that of translating a story into dramatic form. For this a group of children read a carefully chosen story, looking particularly for the sequence of events, characterisation and setting, and they then work as a group to produce their dramatic version of the same story.

The group discussions about what should be included in the play and how they are to portray the characters and their relationships with each other are particularly valuable. It is best if the group is a small one, par-ticularly if children are to work independently of the teacher for most of their discussions and rehearsal; because of this, stories need to be chosen with care for content, readability and the number of characters involved.

This activity has been found to be useful in motivating children to read as they look for more stories to dramatise.

Reading/Listening Activities

These activities include both silent reading by the child as the teacher reads the passage aloud or a tape of the passage is played, and oral reading by the child whilst listening to the teacher or a tape recording. Eventually this might lead to children making their own tape recordings for other members of the class to listen to.

If children are able to listen to a sentence or larger portion of text being read, whilst they follow the print, it helps them to relate the aural and visual symbols of the language, and so aids word recognition, this word recognition being set in a meaningful situation. If children are given the opportunity to listen several times to a short text, they will be able to read all or part of it with their teacher or with a tape of a fluent reader, and will be able to learn to use the important variations of vocal expression. If Reading/Listening Activities are used from an early stage, they can help to avoid the rather stilted reading that some children develop. Alternatively, it can be used to help break a child of a habit of word by word, monotonous reading. This activity can also be used to help to motivate children to read a story for themselves after hearing all or part of the story read by the teacher or on a tape.

Games

Many of the activities already described will be treated by children as games. However, there are many other games which can also aid reading development. A glance through some of the catalogues of educational materials shows the number and variety of games which can be purchased. Many other games can be devised by teachers to meet the particular needs of individual pupils. The following examples are only a selection of the many possibilities.

At the earliest levels of learning to read, various games such as lotto, dominoes and many others can be devised to aid word recognition. Games of the picture-word domino type can also be extended to help children to learn that one word can have more than one meaning, for example, the word 'nut' can be matched to the picture of either a nut from a tree or a nut that screws on to a bolt. Board games are usually popular, and can involve reading words, phrases, or sentences correctly before moving on. Directions such as 'miss a turn' or 'move on six places' always add to the popularity of these games.

Games can be devised to help children to learn particular aspects of reading, for example, syllabification. The syllables of a number of words can be printed on separate cards which are shuffled and dealt to the players.

The first player places one syllable on the table and the next player adds a syllable to this. If players cannot add a syllable from their pile of cards to make a real word they miss a turn. When a word is completed the next player begins a new word. The player with no cards or the fewest cards left, is the winner.

Innumerable games can be devised to teach many different aspects of reading but, whatever game is used, it should have a clear teaching objective and, very importantly, it should be enjoyable for the children. For children who are finding learning to read especially difficult games can be invaluable in giving them extra practice in a form which helps to increase their motivation. More ideas may be found in McNicholas and McEntee (1973) and Nicholson and Williams (1975).

As Hunter-Grundin (1979) points out in her discussion of language games and their uses, games cannot be used as some kind of magic formula to ensure children will learn. The teacher needs to be involved in teaching the children how to use a new game and in evaluating and extending their understanding. Presenting a group of children with a new game and expecting them to play it and learn from it unaided is a recipe for disaster.

Whatever the teaching technique or activity chosen, it is likely to work better with some children than with others, and a variety of carefully chosen activities, each introduced at the appropriate stage of each individual's development, is likely to be more beneficial than a rather monotonous series of similar activities. It is important in choosing an activity that the viewpoint of the child should be taken into consideration; not only should the teacher view the activity as a worthwhile one, but the child should also do so. If thoughtful reading is to be encouraged, care must be taken to choose materials and activities that are worth thinking about. The activities should involve the teacher as well as the pupil in a great deal of thinking.

A final word

In recent years society has been increasingly concerned with 'accountability' in education. There is a general concern, both within schools and in the whole of society, about standards of literacy, particularly as these relate to the needs of industry and commerce. Alongside this debate educators, researchers and theorists are developing a greater depth of understanding of the reading process itself and the ways in which it can best be taught. This development and the increasing demands of society are illustrated in the two definitions of literacy from UNESCO quoted in the Bullock Report (1975, page 10). The first definition dates from 1951, the second from a decade later.

> A person is literate who can, with understanding, both read and write a short, simple statement on his everyday life.

> A person is literate when he has acquired the essential knowledge and skills which enable him to engage in all those activities in which literacy is required for effective functioning in his group and community.

In 1951 many six- or seven-year-olds were literate in terms of the UNESCO definition; with the same standard of achievement in literacy skills, children of the same age would probably not have been considered to be literate ten years later. The second definition is so open-ended that it leaves a feeling of uncertainty about when a person can be described as literate, since the demands made on the individual in terms of reading are constantly changing and a standard of literacy that may fulfil someone's needs today may be insufficient in the future. Perhaps it is appropriate to talk of literacy only in terms of specific tasks rather than as a total, once and for all achievement.

The dilemma for the primary school teacher is that society demands that children be educated in terms of the needs of society and the needs of young people as they leave school. Predicting exactly what those needs will be five to thirteen years hence, when pupils will be leaving school is extremely difficult, if not impracticable and some might say unethical since the needs of some children might be underestimated.

Perhaps a more worthwhile approach would be for teachers to consider themselves to be 'accountable' to the individual child, and to teach children according to their needs at present, ensuring at the same time that they gain a sound basis of helpful attitudes, useful skills and knowledge upon which they can build, and that above all they are inspired with enthusiasm and purpose for reading, and are encouraged to become independent readers both at the functional and the critical level; in this way they are likely to develop into readers who can and do read for whatever purpose they have or society demands.

Appendix 1

Suggested notation for recording oral reading miscues

Omissions	John ask⊘if he went (to)(his) home.
Insertions	The boy went to ∧school. (*the* inserted)
Pauses	I went to the‖circus.
Words sounded letter by letter	mountain
Substitutions	house The horse went up the road.
Self-corrections	c up Up and⌐down went the swing.

Appendix 2

Informal check-lists

Pre-reading stage

Name .... Date of Birth ....

Dates of assessments						
Has an understanding of what reading is and its uses						
Attitudes Is eager to learn to read						

Intellectual Skills
Understands that a picture represents an object or event
Communicates effectively orally
Understands vocabulary of materials to be used
Understands the terms (i) word
                 (ii) sound
               (iii) letter
Can memorise a short poem or song
Can predict the ending of a story told to him/her
Can sequence a series of pictures to form a story
Can view items in order from left to right
Can repeat words/sounds demonstrated
Can select two identical shapes/letters from a group of similar ones						

Work Habits
Works well in a group
Attends to what other
     (i) children say
     (ii) adults say
Normally completes work set
Can concentrate on one piece of work for 5–10 minutes						

Suggested 5 point scale for marking check-lists:
 (1) poor level/absent
 (2) not very good
 (3) fair
 (4) good
 (5) excellent/skillfully attained

Early Reading Stage
Name .... Date of birth ....

Dates of assessments						
Has an understanding of what reading is and its uses						
Attitudes Chooses to read voluntarily Able to discuss likes/dislikes about material read Enjoys reading materials used for instruction Shows signs of stress during reading						

Intellectual Skills
Can answer literal questions
Can answer inferential questions
Can predict how a story will continue
Can retell in own words what has been read
Word recognition strategies used:
    (i) semantic context
    (ii) syntactic context
    (iii) phonics
    (iv) configuration
Word recognition strategies are used effectively together
Is able to self-correct
Appropriate use of illustrations
Understands vocabulary of materials read
Understands sentence structures used
Oral reading: (i) reads with good expression
    (ii) observes punctuation marks
    (iii) has confidence in reading to an audience						

Work Habits Listens attentively to others Able to concentrate on a task and complete it independently						
Physical Well-being Shows signs of tiredness Vision appears normal Hearing appears normal General health good						

The Competent Primary School Reader

Name .... Date of Birth ....

Dates of assessments						
Attitudes Has positive attitudes towards reading Enjoys reading the material used for instruction Reads voluntarily Shows signs of stress during reading						

Intellectual Skills
Has effective word recognition strategies
Can answer literal questions
Can answer inferential questions
Can answer evaluative questions
Can discuss likes/dislikes of material (plot,
   characters, style, etc.)
Can find the main idea of a text
Can set appropriate purposes and questions
   for reading
Can find an appropriate text efficiently
Can use a table of contents
Can use an index
Can use a dictionary
Makes effective use of reading:
  (i) memorises useful material
  (ii) follows directions
  (iii) takes notes
  (iv) draws diagrams
  (v) completes a task using reading as an aid
  (vi) Takes part in a discussion about material
    read
Oral reading:
  (i) reads with good expression
  (ii) observes punctuation marks
  (iii) has confidence in reading to an audience						

Work Habits Attends well to work Works well in a group Works independently Shows initiative						
Physical Well-being Shows signs of tiredness Vision appears normal Hearing appears normal General health good						

These check-lists are by no means exhaustive of all the items which could be included; however, if all the possible items were to be included, it is doubtful if the check-list could ever be administered or used, as it would become so unwieldy. A fairly short check-list or the use of part of a check-list is of far more value, since it is always possible for a teacher to observe an area of apparent difficulty in more detail if required.

Bibliography

ARNOLD, H. (1982) *Listening to Children Reading*. London: Hodder and Stoughton.

AUSUBEL, D. P. (1963) 'Reception learning and the rote-meaningful dimension' in STONES, E. (ed.) (1970) *Readings in Educational Psychology: Learning and Teaching*. London: Methuen.

BARR, R. (1975) 'The Effect of instruction on pupil reading strategies' in *Reading Research Quarterly*, **10**, 4, pp. 555–82.

BARRETT, T. C. (1968) 'Taxonomy of cognitive and affective dimensions of reading comprehension' in ROBINSON, H. M. (ed.) (1963) *Innovation and Change in Reading Instruction*. Chicago, Ill.: University of Chicago Press.

BIEMILLER, A. (1970) 'The development of the use of graphic and contextual information as children learn to read' in *Reading Research Quarterly*, **6**, 1.

BRUCE, D. J. (1964) 'The analysis of word sounds by young children' in *British Journal of Educational Psychology*, **34**, 2, pp. 158–70.

BRUNER, J. S. (1973) *Beyond the Information Given*. London: George Allen and Unwin.

BULLOCK, SIR A. (ed.) (1975) *A Language for Life* (The Bullock Report). London: HMSO.

BURKE, E. (1976) 'A developmental study of children's reading strategies' in *Educational Review*, **29**, 1, pp. 30–46.

COHEN, A. S. (1975) 'Oral reading errors of first grade children taught by a code emphasis approach' in *Reading Research Quarterly*, **10**, 4, pp. 616–50.

DOWNING, J. (1970) 'Children's concepts of language in learning to read' in *Educational Research*, **12**, 2, pp. 106–112.

FINN, J. D. (1972) 'Expectations and the educational environment' in *Review of Educational Research*, **42**, 3, pp. 387–410.

GOODMAN, K. S. (1965) 'A linguistic study of cues and miscues in reading' in *Elementary English*, 42, pp. 639–43.

GOODMAN, K. S. (1969) 'Analysis of oral reading miscues: applied psycholinguistics' in *Reading Research Quarterly*, 5.

GREGORY, O. (1979) *Oxford Junior English*. Oxford: Oxford University Press.

HOFFMAN, M. (1976) *Reading, Writing and Relevance*. London: Hodder and Stoughton.

HUNTER-GRUNDIN, E. (1979) *Literacy: a Systematic Start.* New York: Harper and Row.

LUNZER, E. and GARDNER, K. (1979) *The Effective Use of Reading.* London: Heinemann Educational for the Schools Council.

MCCULLOUGH, C. M. (1957) 'Responses of elementary school children to common types of reading comprehension question' in *Journal of Educational Research*, 51, pp. 65–70.

MCNICHOLAS, J. and MCENTEE, J. (1973) *Games to Develop Reading Skills.* Stafford: National Association for Remedial Education.

MACKAY, D. *et al.* (1970) *Breakthrough to Literacy.* Harlow: Longman.

MELNIK, A. and MERRITT, J. E. (1972) *Reading: Today and Tomorrow.* London: Hodder and Stoughton.

MERRITT, J. E. (1973) *Perspectives on Reading.* Milton Keynes: Open University Press.

MERRITT, J. E. (1974) *What Shall We Teach?* London: Ward Lock Educational.

MERRITT, J. E. (1978) 'Who is Literate?' in MCCULLOUGH, C. M. (ed.) (1980) *Inchworm, Inchworm: Persistent Problems in Reading Education.* Newark, Del.: International Reading Association.

MOON, C. (1977) *Individualized Reading.* Reading: University of Reading, Centre for the Teaching of Reading.

MOYLE, D. (1976) 'Sequence and Structure in Reading Development' in MERRITT, J. E. (ed.) *New Horizons in Reading.* Newark, Del.: International Reading Association.

NICHOLSON, D. and WILLIAMS, G. (1975) *Word Games for the Teaching of Reading.* London: Pitman Books.

OPEN UNIVERSITY (1977) *Reading Development* (Block 2). Milton Keynes: Open University Press.

PALARDY, J. M. (1969) 'What teachers believe: what children achieve' in *Elementary School Journal.*

PIDGEON, D. A. (1970) *Expectation and Pupil Performance.* Slough: NFER.

PILLAR, A. (1982) 'Evoking creative responses to literature from students at elementary and middle school levels' in HENDRY, A. (ed.) *Teaching Reading: the Key Issues.* London: Heinemann Educational.

PARKER, D. (1969) *SRA International Reading Laboratory.* London: SRA Associates.

PUMFREY, P. D. (1976) *Reading: Tests and Assessment Techniques.* London: Hodder and Stoughton.

REID, J. F. (1972) *Reading Problems and Practices.* London: Ward Lock Educational.

ROSE, J. E., MALIS, L. I. and BAKER, C. P. (1961) 'Neural Growth in the Cerebral Cortex after Lesions Produced by Monoenergetic Deuterons' in PRIBAM, H. K. (ed.) (1969) *Brain and Behaviour 3, Memory Mechanisms*. Harmondsworth: Penguin.

ROSENTHAL, R. and JACOBSON, L. (1968) *Pygmalion in the Classroom. Teacher Expectation and Pupils' Intellectual Development*. New York: Holt, Rinehart and Winston.

SINGER, H. (1978) 'Active Comprehension: From answering to asking questions' in *The Reading Teacher*, **31**, 8, pp. 901–8.

SMITH, F. (1978) *Reading*. Cambridge: Cambridge University Press.

SOUTHGATE, V., ARNOLD, H. and JOHNSON, S. (1981) *Extending Beginning Reading*. London: Heinemann Educational for the Schools Council.

STAUFFER, R. G. (1969) *Learning to Read as a Thinking Process*. London: Harper and Row.

STAUFFER, R. G. (1970) *Directing Reading Maturity as a Cognitive Process*. London: Harper and Row.

STAUFFER, R. G. 'Cognitive Processes Fundamental to Reading Instruction' in GUTHRIE, J. T. (ed.) (1977) *Cognition, Curriculum and Comprehension*. Newark, Del.: International Reading Association.

STRANG, R. (1969) 'Informal Reading Inventories' in MELNIK, A. and MERRITT, J. E. (eds) (1972) *The Reading Curriculum*. London: University of London Press Ltd.

THORNDIKE, E. L. (1917) 'Reading as Reasoning: a study of mistakes in paragraph reading' in MELNIK, A. and MERRITT, J. E. (eds) (1972) *Reading: Today and Tomorrow*. London: Hodder and Stoughton.

TURNER, J. (1976) *The Assessment of Reading Skills*. Ormskirk: UKRA.

WILSON, E. (1977) *The GPID Strategies of a Group of Third Year Junior Children*. Unpublished dissertation. Edge Hill College of Higher Education.

Index